T0191391

ARTIFICIAL
INTELLIGENCE

ARTIFICIAL INTELLIGENCE

FROM MACHINE LEARNING TO SUPER-INTELLIGENCE AND THE SINGULARITY

RICHARD URWIN

SIRIUS

SIRIUS

This edition published in 2024 by Sirius Publishing, a division of
Arcturus Publishing Limited,
26/27 Bickels Yard, 151–153 Bermondsey Street,
London SE1 3HA

ISBN: 978-1-3988-4202-1
AD012061UK

Printed in China

CONTENTS

CHAPTER 1

What is Artificial Intelligence?

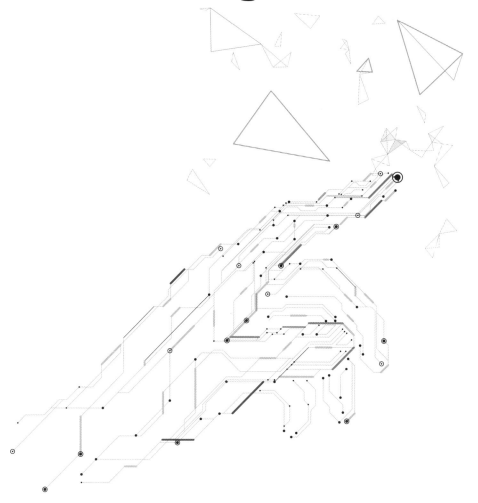

One of the features that distinguishes humanity from other animals is the use of labour-saving devices. We invented the wheel and the lever so that we didn't have to carry heavy loads for long distances. We invented the spear so that we didn't have to kill our dinner with our bare hands. For many thousands of years we have been developing ever more complex machinery to save ourselves physical effort and yet, for all that time, a device that saves us from mental drudgery has been little more than a distant dream.

There have been a few tools over the centuries that somewhat eased our mental labour, such as the slide rule and the adding machine, but such things are specialized to very narrow applications. Only recently have we had the technology to begin to explore a general-purpose thinking machine.

It is early days yet.

The computer is less than 100 years old and the subject is exceptionally complex – but we are now beginning to see the fruits of our labour. Artificial intelligence is now part of many devices that we use every day. When we ask our phone what the time is in Seattle, that's artificial intelligence. When we are playing a video game and a computer-controlled monster sneaks around and stabs us in the back, that's artificial intelligence. AI invests our pensions on the stock market and it refuses us a loan. It can even vacuum our floors.

The search is not yet over. These are merely the first products of our research, but – as artificial intelligence becomes ever more pervasive – we have to understand what it is and what it is not if we are to make sense of our world.

Before we can describe artificial intelligence, we need to define what we are talking about. It seems obvious that artificial intelligence is intelligence that is artificial, but unfortunately neither of those words has a clear definition. For example, if a magician were to conjure a brain out of thin air, would that be counted as an artificial intelligence? Even if it were, it is doubtful that we could say anything meaningful about it. By intelligent, do we mean a mind that is self-aware and can ponder the meaning of life as well as any human? In that case this book would be very short, since no such thing has been invented and nobody has more than the faintest idea how it might be achieved.

'Artificial'

In this book we will say that the intelligence must be man-made – by which we mean that it must be a product of science and engineering. No magic is allowed.

Similarly, biology is disallowed in our discussion: genetic engineering shares no science with the fields we will be discussing. Brain cells have been grown in Petri dishes but they can only be understood either as part of a natural brain or so far as they match the simplified versions that we implement in our computers.

For any mechanism or electronic circuit that can be designed, the same principles can be implemented in a computer program.

And, while you need a machine shop or an electronics lab – plus a significant budget – to create a mechanism or circuit of this kind, the equivalent computer program can be produced quickly and cheaply by an undergraduate student.

This is why all artificial intelligence research is carried out using computers. All the technologies we will be discussing in this book are implemented on computers.

'Intelligence'

Intelligence presents a rather more difficult choice. As a human, it is difficult to imagine intelligence without also imagining consciousness.

That part of us that experiences being alive and having an identity seems to be removed from purely physical processes. We can see that some people are cleverer than others and we can accept that their brains are responsible for that; but the experience of existing seems to be universal. It is difficult to imagine that such a thing could be generated by a mere machine. In fact it is an article of faith for us all that any human apart from ourselves experiences living in the same way we do. And only in the last few decades have people begun to believe that other animals might also be conscious.

We can never know what another being thinks – whether human, animal or machine. There is no test for consciousness. If a machine ever developed consciousness, we could never know. Philosophers have been arguing for centuries over what it means to think or to be self-aware and they have not come to any firm conclusions.

We believe we may be able to create a machine that displays all of the outward signs of being intelligent. But one with consciousness, free will and the ability to think? We will come back to these issues later. Until then we will limit ourselves to discussing those outward signs of intelligence that we can observe and measure. Even here the choice is not clear; our understanding of intelligence has changed over time.

In 1906, French psychologist Alfred Binet defined intelligence as: '...judgement, otherwise called good sense, practical sense, initiative, the faculty of adapting one's self to circumstances. To judge well, to comprehend well, to reason well...But memory is distinct from and independent of judgement.'[1]

However, the tests for intelligence that Binet went on to propose depended on a knowledge of human culture: his fourth test is the recognition of familiar food and his sixth assesses the ability of the subject to understand shaking hands. A person with no memory would do very badly at such tasks, as would someone from a different culture.

It is impossible to operate in the real world without knowledge about how it works. From our very first moments of life we start to create this vast store of information and it

---

1 Alfred Binet, 'New Methods for the Diagnosis of the Intellectual Level of Subnormals.' First published in *L'Année Psychologique*, 12 (1905): 191–244. This translation, by Elizabeth S. Kite, first appeared in 1916 in *The Development of Intelligence in Children* (Vineland, NJ: Publications of the Training School at Vineland).

French psychologist, Alfred Binet.

takes more than ten years, maybe more than 20, for it to be completed. A computer program that took so long to become useful would be nearly pointless.

The Oxford English Dictionary now defines intelligence as "the ability to acquire and apply knowledge and skills",[2] which clearly depends on memory. It may be that the field of artificial intelligence has affected our understanding of intelligence in general so that we now see how important knowledge is in allowing us to apply judgement to our situation. Getting this knowledge into a computer and storing it in a manner that allows the computer to make use of it is a major field of artificial intelligence that we will be investigating in due course.

There is a fundamental problem that has dogged artificial intelligence since its inception. If computers can do it, then it obviously isn't something that requires intelligence.

One of the first problems that programmers worked on was the game of chess. Here, they thought, was something at which only a human could excel. In 1997, the IBM machine Deep Blue beat Garry Kasparov, the reigning grandmaster. But Deep Blue was not displaying any human attributes; it was merely very fast and very efficiently programmed for that single task.

Turing Test

Back in 1950, soon after computers were invented, the English mathematician Alan Turing proposed a test for machine

2 Oxford Dictionaries, accessed 7 January, 2016, www.oxforddictionaries.com

intelligence that became known as the Turing Test. In an experiment a computer and a human both converse with an examiner for five minutes and then the examiner has to decide which is which. Turing judged that by the year 2000 the examiner would only be right 70 per cent of the time. There is an annual competition (called the Loebner Prize) for the program that is the most human-like out of all the entrants. So far no program has performed as well as Turing predicted,[3] but they are getting better all the time. Just as chess programs can now beat grandmasters, computers will eventually converse with the same fluency as humans. When they do so, it will become immediately apparent that conversational skill is no proof of intelligence. That is a problem because we can never know what another being is thinking. Communication is all we have.

Strong AI

There are three approaches to artificial intelligence. Proponents of Strong AI believe that it is possible to build a machine that thinks in the same way a human thinks – that it would be possible

---

3 Other than the Loebner Prize, there have been a few programs that exceeded the 30 per cent threshold that Turing predicted. The most famous of these is Eugene Goostman, a program that pretended to be a 13-year-old boy because the program's mistakes could then be blamed on the boy's teenage attitude, sense of humour and limited English skills. It fooled 33 per cent of the judges but you wouldn't want it programmed into your sat-nav. See Doug Aamoth, 'Interview with Eugene Goostman, the Fake Kid Who Passed the Turing Test', *Time*, 9 June, 2014, accessed 29 January, 2016, http://time.com/2847900/eugene-goostman-turing-test/.

to say that the machine understands information and is conscious. As we have seen, it would be difficult to prove such a thing. In order to create a computer program that we are sure has Strong AI we would have to understand exactly how the human mind works – and we are still a long way from that.

Weak AI

For Weak AI on the other hand, it is only necessary for the machine to behave as if it is intelligent. The implementation details are unimportant. Such thinking led to Deep Blue, but Deep Blue did not even attempt to mimic the mind of a chess grandmaster; it merely followed rules about which moves it should make. If a human attempted to follow the same rules as the computer then the game would last a very long time, since the computer was examining 200 million possible positions per second. Even given the prodigious minds of grandmasters, it is unlikely that they could do the same. A human seems to use a more highly developed strategic sense that limits the number of positions they have to consider to something of the order of dozens, maybe several dozens – but not millions. In Weak AI this distinction is of no importance; the fact that the computer can play chess better than a human is all that matters.

Pragmatic AI

There is a third approach that I will call Pragmatic AI. Instead of trying to create a machine that is as intelligent as a human, researchers set their sights lower.

We now know how to create robots that behave like insects. It may seem of little use to have a robotic housefly, especially one as large as a shoebox, but there are tasks for which even such a robot could prove useful. Maybe a swarm of robots the size of dogs but with the intelligence of ants would be very useful clearing rubble and searching for survivors in disaster areas.

Eventually, as our models become more sophisticated and our machines mimic ever more complex creatures, there may come a point at which our machines appear to be as intelligent as a human. It may be that this approach is the same as Strong AI. But it is not necessary for us to believe that the robots we build are conscious and, by the time we have added all that complexity, we may no longer be certain that we are mimicking real life. We may only be able to say that they are indistinguishable from a machine that is conscious.

A definition

For the purposes of this book we will say that an artificial intelligence is a tool constructed to aid or substitute for human thought. It is a computer program, whether standing alone in a data centre or a PC or embodied in a device such as a robot, which displays the outward signs of being intelligent – those signs being the ability to acquire and apply knowledge and skills in order to act with reason in its environment.

CHAPTER 2

Tools for Thinking – First Steps Towards AI?

The roots of artificial intelligence go much deeper than the first electronic computers. For centuries, humans have used tools to help them think.

Maybe the first of these were small pebbles: a shepherd could have the same number of stones in a bag as he had sheep; when he wanted to make sure that his stock was all present all he had to do was take out one stone for each sheep – if there were still stones left in the bag then he had a missing animal.

Once stones meant numbers, it would have been a small step for a different sort of stone to mean five, ten, 12 or 20. The counting boards that were ubiquitous in the Middle Ages are direct descendants. In other places, the same ideas produced the forerunners to the modern abacus. Eventually, our continued reliance on calculative tools would lead to the creation of the modern pocket calculator.

Standing stones

Counting was not the only mental task that ancient people mechanized. We know that Stonehenge and other such monuments marked midwinter and midsummer. We also know that they could have predicted eclipses and other astronomical events, as well. The numbers are there in the structures. For example, there are 19 stones in a horseshoe-shaped arrangement in the middle of the monument, and it takes 19 years for the

Sun and Moon to repeat their positions. Knowing what we do today, we could use them to predict eclipses by moving tokens from stone to stone each month. Eclipses are erratic events, depending on several cycles of different lengths coinciding at particular times. Predicting them takes a lot of painstaking calculation and a tool that kept track of these cycles would have been invaluable.

Unfortunately, there is no evidence that the stone circles were ever used in this way. If they were we might expect that some remnant tradition would have survived. But none has. It seems most likely that the number of stones in these monuments were chosen only to display sacred knowledge. If the priests had other tools to help them calculate, and it is possible that they did, none of them have survived.

The Antikythera mechanism

In 1900, a group of sponge divers operating near the Greek island of Antikythera found the remains of a Roman ship lying more than 45 metres (145 feet) below the surface. The government was informed and archaeologists worked on the wreck for a year, recovering many objects. Among these finds were metallic pieces that were tentatively identified as an astrolabe. To describe them as heavily corroded is an understatement; they may be better described as lumps of corrosion with the impression of parts of dials on the surface.

The mechanism was slow to give up its secrets. X-rays taken in 1951 proved it was more complex than originally thoughts

A fragment of the Antikythera mechanism,
which dates from 150–100 BCE.

but it was not until the 21st century that technology has been available to discern the detailed design of the mechanism. That process is still ongoing.

The mechanism appears to date from 150–100 BCE. It contained at least 36 handmade gears. Simply by setting its date dial it predicted the positions of the Sun and Moon, and the rising and setting of certain stars. It could be used to predict eclipses, since the 19-year cycle is engraved as a spiral on one of the pieces. The likelihood is that it also displayed the position of the five planets that were known at the time. Not for another thousand years were mechanisms of comparable complexity made. This must have been a highly valuable device and its operation would have seemed almost magical. Simply by turning the handle, one could watch the heavens revolve.

Pygmalion

In 8 CE the Roman poet Ovid finished his 15-book epic poem *Metamorphoses*. This includes (in Book X, Fable VII) the story of Pygmalion who, disgusted at the decadent behaviour of the women around him, constructs an ivory statue and falls in love with it. He treats it as his wife, dressing it and hanging jewellery on it. He even takes it to bed with him. Then on a festival of Venus he prays: 'If ye gods can grant all things, let my wife be, I pray, like to this statue of ivory.' Venus hears his prayer and when he returns to the statue it turns to living flesh under his caresses. It would be wrong to ascribe to this story the root of interest in artificial intelligence; it clearly has other meanings, but it does indicate that the idea of creating living beings from inanimate matter was not an inconceivable concept at the time.

Arabic numerals

There is an apocryphal tale of a German merchant of around the 13th century telling his son that if all he wished was to learn to add and subtract, a German university would be sufficient, but if he wanted to know multiplication and division then he must go to Italy. The human intellect has not changed in any great degree in thousands of years, if not tens of thousands, so what made simple arithmetic so hard? At that time all numbers were written in Roman numerals. One only has to consider the difficulty of multiplying VI by VII and making XLII to realize that calculating on paper as we do today was all but impossible. Such complex operations were carried out on counting boards. These were tables with a grid marked on the surface. There were columns for units, tens, hundreds and so forth. Counters were placed on the board and calculations carried out by following rules, much the same as our long division or multiplication. The boards made arithmetic possible but, as the above tale makes clear, never easy.

The answer to these difficulties had been invented in India several centuries before. Indian mathematicians used a single set of ten digits with the position of the digit within the number defining whether it was the number of units, tens, hundreds and so forth, as we do today. When we read '234' we know that we have two hundreds, three tens and four units.

This new concept travelled west through Arabia to Europe, at each stage being met with distrust and disdain. The difficulty was the digit zero, which had almost never been used before. Sometimes it stood for nothing, as when it came before a digit – 03 is the same as 3. But at others it multiplied a digit by ten or a hundred or more – 30 is not the same as 3. With Roman numerals every character always had the same definite value; I was always one and X was always ten. Zero was not even counted as a digit at first; it was outside the digits, it was something else, something alien. In time, however, the advantage of the new method was so great that it eventually replaced the old and in doing so greatly enhanced the speed and complexity of calculations that could be carried out.

Golem

The Talmud (the Jewish religious and legal document first written down c.200–500 CE) contains a few descriptions of golems – creatures created from dirt and animated by religious ritual. Around 1100 CE this caught the interest of Jewish scholars and stories of golems became current. The *Sefer Yezirah*,[4] the

4 Rev. Dr Isidor Kalisch, *Sepher Yezirah. A Book on Creation; or, The Jewish Metaphysics of Remote Antiquity*. With English Translation, Preface, Explanatory Notes and Glossary (New York, 1877: L.H. Frank & Co). There is a version available online at the Sacred Texts website, accessed 7 January, 2016, http://www.sacred-texts.com/jud/sy/sy00.htm

'Book of Creation', is said to contain the instructions for creating a golem. This tome is nothing more than an account of the creation and its relation to the Hebrew alphabet; there is nothing in it that says, 'This is how to make a golem'. But constructing such a beast was understood as an act of creation using the same technique that God had used when he created Adam from dust.

The general method settled on by legend was to create a human shape from earth and place on or in it a word in Hebrew text – the letters and words of which are believed to have spiritual power. The name of God was a popular choice. To destroy the golem one had only to remove or erase the letters and the creature would return to the dust from which it was made.

The most famous of golem legends is that of the Golem of Prague, said to have been created by Rabbi Loew (1520–1609) who, on hearing that anti-Jewish sentiment was being drummed up, prayed to God for help. As answer to his prayer he received the instructions for creating a golem. He created a giant body from river clay and walked seven times around it one way and seven times the other way reciting verses from the Torah before putting a paper with the full name of God in its mouth and pronouncing the final verse. The golem then came to life and protected the Jewish community. When its task was complete, the rabbi removed the paper from its mouth and the creature returned to clay. The body was said to have been stored in the attic of the synagogue in case it was ever needed again.

To modern computer scientists, another of the various methods of creating a golem is more interesting. In order to bring the creation to life, rather than the name of God, one wrote the word תמא, *emet*, meaning 'truth'. In addition to truth being a succinct expression of the concept of divinity, these are the last letters of the last three words in the account of the Creation in Genesis 2:3. The words can be understood to be an instruction to humankind to continue the acts that Creation had begun: 'God created to do'.[5] It was an instruction to live, as delivered from God Himself. We can compare this to the modern robot, which contains within it instructions for how it should act. When the golem had outlasted its usefulness, one merely erased the first letter, א, (Hebrew is written from right to left), leaving תמ, *met*, meaning 'death'. The instruction to live was replaced with the instruction to die. This may be the first ever example of software hacking.

Frankenstein

No list of the precursors of artificial intelligence machines would be complete without mentioning Mary Shelley's *Frankenstein*. This novel – full title, *Frankenstein: or, The*

---

5 This was a valid reading of those words at that time – such are the difficulties of translating and understanding colloquial Hebrew that was written thousands of years ago. The words are probably more correctly translated as in the New International Version of the Bible: 'all the work of creating that he had done'. See Bible Gateway, accessed 7 January, 2016, https://www.biblegateway.com/passage/?search=Genesis%202-3

Modern Prometheus – was begun in 1816 while the 18 year-old Mary Godwin was travelling through Europe with her lover Percy Shelley and her stepsister Claire Clairmont.

Claire, also 18, was complicit in Mary and Shelley's illicit affair and was herself passionately enamoured of the poet George Gordon, Lord Byron. Byron did not return her love but he had taken advantage of it and Claire was pregnant with his child. Byron himself had recently left England in the face of scandal surrounding his relationship with his half-sister and various ladies of ill repute that had caused his wife to leave him and take their daughter Ada with her.

That summer Shelley's party stayed with Byron and his doctor, John Polidori, by Lake Geneva. It was in this crucible that the story of Frankenstein was forged.

Unlike the golem of Jewish myth, Frankenstein's monster was created from parts gathered from the dissecting room and the slaughterhouse. Although Shelley does not tell how it is brought to life (the lightning bolts beloved of film adaptations are not in the original), it is clearly achieved by science rather than mysticism.

Frankenstein's creation was monstrous in aspect: 'His yellow skin scarcely covered the work of muscles and arteries beneath; his hair was of a lustrous black, and flowing; his teeth of a pearly whiteness; but these luxuriances only formed a more horrid contrast with his watery eyes, that seemed almost of the same colour as the dun-white sockets in which they were set, his shrivelled complexion and straight black lips.[6]

Nevertheless it was intelligent and well-spoken. This was not a mute subhuman like the golem, nor even the grunting monster of film but a thinking and caring person, albeit one who committed murders.

Babbage and his mathematical engines

Only five years after the publication of *Frankenstein*, English mathematician and inventor Charles Babbage began work on the first of the engines that were to consume much of his time for the rest of his life.

At that time, complex calculations were not computed on the spot – as we may now do with a pocket calculator or with a smartphone application. Attempting to do so then would have taken many minutes with a pencil and paper, with many opportunities for error. Rather, tables were printed so that you could, for example, find the necessary repayment rate of a loan at a given interest percentage or the required elevation and load of a gun for a given range. Since these tables had to be prepared by hand, then typeset by hand, they were in their turn beset with errors.

6 Mary Wollstonecraft (Godwin) Shelley, *Frankenstein, or The Modern Prometheus*. The book is available online at Project Gutenberg, accessed 7 January, 2016, https://www.gutenberg.org/ or in print

The Difference Engine built by the London Science Museum between 1985 and 2002.

While Babbage with his friend John Herschel was engaged in the painstaking process of checking such tables he lamented that they were not calculated by steam. And in due course this is what he set out to achieve.

Difference Engine

The machine he created, with funding from the British government, was the Difference Engine. It was not a computer as we know it, since it was only capable of handling the single calculation necessary to compile such a table. It was to be a huge structure, weighing some 3.6 tonnes (4 tons). However, Babbage fell into disagreement with the craftsman making the parts and it was never completed. The government, out of pocket by £17,500, lost faith in the endeavour and only a fraction of the engine was ever completed.

At around the time that work ceased on the Difference Engine, Babbage met the 17-year-old mathematician Ada Byron – daughter of the poet Lord Byron – and was struck by her mathematical skills. He invited her to see the Difference Engine, such as it was, and she was fascinated by the machine. The two corresponded thereafter and Babbage affectionately dubbed her the 'Enchantress of Number'. Ada later married William King who became the Earl of Lovelace.

It is as Ada, Countess of Lovelace[7] that she is known today.

Analytical Engine

Babbage now continued to work, not on his Difference Engine, but on an altogether grander project he called the Analytical Engine. This was to be a mechanical computer, programmed with punched cards like those used by the Jacquard loom[8] and capable of any mathematical calculation. In 1842, Babbage asked Ada to translate an article about the engine from French to English and to add further notes of her own. These notes contain a program for the engine that has the distinction of being the first computer program to be published; Ada Lovelace is now known as the first computer programmer. It is certain that she understood the engine as well as anyone other than Babbage himself. Nevertheless, she doubted that the engine would lead to anything that could be termed intelligent. She wrote: "The Analytical Engine has no pretensions whatever to originate anything. It can do whatever we know how to order it to perform. It can follow analysis; but it has no power of

---

7 The wife of an earl is a countess. There are no counts in the British peerage. As a daughter of Baron Byron she was addressed as The Honourable Ada Byron. Her husband was already a baron when she married him and to confuse matters further he had the surname King. She was then addressed as Lady Ada King. When her husband was made Earl of Lovelace, she was addressed as 'Ada, Countess of Lovelace'.

8 The Jacquard loom was first demonstrated in 1801. It was the first device to use cards punched with holes to hold information. In this case each hole (or its absence) corresponded to a set of warp threads that were lifted (or not) for each weft thread. It allowed intricate designs to be created and reproduced in any quantity.

anticipating any analytical relations or truths. Its province is to assist us in making available what we are already acquainted with."[9]

The Analytical Engine was never built, nor even designed in full. It exists only as a series of partial diagrams. However, while working on these, Babbage also created a new design for a Difference Engine using principles and improvements drawn from the Analytical Engine. Although there were no funds to build it at the time, this second Difference Engine was constructed at the London Science Museum between 1985 and 2002 from Babbage's designs, using materials and tolerances achievable in the 19th century. It works as Babbage intended.

Rosumovi Univerzální Roboti

Having spent 400 years in England, we travel back to the land of the golem for Karel Čapek's *R.U.R.*, a play first performed in 1920. The title stands for *Rosumovi Univerzální Roboti* – in English, *Rossum's Universal Robots*. This is the source of the word 'robot', which is derived from the old Czech word *robota*,[10] meaning forced labour. The robots in the play are not mechan-

---

9 *Sketch of The Analytical Engine Invented by Charles Babbage* by L.F. Menabrea of Turin, Officer of the Military Engineers from the *Bibliothèque Universelle de Genève*, October, 1842, No. 82 With notes upon the Memoir by the Translator Ada Augusta, Countess of Lovelace in *Bibliothèque Universelle de Genève*, October 1842, No. 82. It is available online, accessed 7 January, 2016, http://www.fourmilab.ch/babbage/sketch.html .

10 The word *robota* is no longer used in modern Czech, except in a small area in the northeast of the Czech Republic. It is still in current use in Slovak and Russian.

ical devices but created biological creatures, albeit devoid of emotion. Science had advanced again since Frankenstein but these creations appear less human at first than did the monster. It is only at the end – after destroying the human race – that they develop the ability to love.

Second World War

Global conflict focused the minds of a generation of mathematicians on the problem of performing complex mathematical processes as quickly as possible. Both sides in the conflict sent orders and strategic information by radio and these signals were also received by their enemies. Such signals were encrypted to prevent the enemy understanding them. Breaking the enemy's codes often meant life or death for hundreds of people. Automating these processes had obvious benefits. By the end of the war there were two machines that could be seen as the parents of the modern computer. The United States had the Electronic Numerical Integrator And Computer (ENIAC) and the United Kingdom had Colossus.

Neither of these machines was capable of being programmed as we know it today. Configuring them for a new task involved moving wires around and turning switches. But the knowledge gained by building them allowed the first real computers to be built only three years after the end of the war.

These early computers, such as the Small-Scale

Experimental Machine (SSEM)[11] and the Electronic Discrete Variable Automatic Computer (EDVAC)[12], were true computers. They were general-purpose, capable of running any program. Moreover, they held that program in their memory.

It was less than two years after these computers first ran that Alan Turing was able to write: 'I believe that at the end of the century the use of words and general educated opinion will have altered so much that one will be able to speak of machines thinking without expecting to be contradicted.'[13] The tools and the mindset were all in place. Research into artificial intelligence could now begin.

11 The Small-Scale Experimental Machine was built at Manchester University in the UK. It ran its first program in July 1948.

12 The Electronic Discrete Variable Automatic Computer was built at the US Army's Ballistics Research Laboratory in Aberdeen, Maryland, United States, August 1949.

13 A.M. Turing, 'Computing Machinery and Intelligence', *Mind: A Quarterly Review of Psychology and Philosophy* (October 1950): 433–60. The paper is available in several places on the Internet, including in the *Mind* back-catalogue at http://mind.oxfordjournals.org/; or try the Loebner Prize website at http://www.loebner.net/Prizef/TuringArticle.html. The paper is readable and thought provoking: I recommend interested readers to search it out.

CHAPTER 3

The Computer

Before we examine artificial intelligence, we should take a moment to understand the technology that makes it possible. All the concepts with which we will be engaging in later chapters are computer programs and this has far-reaching consequences.

The word 'computer' was not invented in the 1940s. Before the Zuse Z3,[14] the EDVAC and the SSEM, a computer was a person employed to do computation. These human computers would sit at their desk all day with a sheet of paper, a printed instruction sheet and maybe a mechanical adding machine. They would painstakingly work through the instructions, step by step, and produce a result. If they were careful enough, the result would be right.

During the Second World War, computers were built for specific tasks. Like the Difference Engine, they only carried out a single computation. If the job changed, someone had to design a new computer. To make the task easier, machines such as the Electronic Numerical Integrator and Computer (ENIAC)[15] were

14 The Zuse Z3 was built in Germany during the Second World War and was more advanced as a computer than anything the Allies had. It was a true general-purpose computer and differed from modern machines only in that its program was held on paper tape rather than in memory. It was destroyed by an Allied air raid on Berlin in 1943.

15 The Electronic Numerical Integrator and Computer was built for the US Army Ordnance Corps and spent most of its time calculating artillery tables, although it also worked on calculations integral to the mathematics behind the hydrogen bomb.

made. ENIAC was composed of a collection of parts that could be wired together in various combinations to carry out different computations. Building a new computer now involved simply rewiring the one machine.

Back in 1936, Alan Turing had proved that any sufficiently powerful computer could pretend to be any other computer. By sufficiently powerful, he meant theoretically be able to carry out any calculation of which mathematics is capable, with the understanding that memory and time requirements might make some of them impossible in practice. Such machines are described as 'Turing complete'.

If you had such a computer then all you would have to do to create a new computer would be to provide new data to the single real machine. No moving of wires or turning of switches would be required.

A few months after the SSEM ran its first program, ENIAC was extended to make it possible to configure it to do just this: ENIAC, a machine without a stored program and with 20 accumulators and no memory, was emulating a computer that had a stored program, one accumulator and 16 memory locations. The computer it was emulating never existed; it was entirely imaginary. The SSEM, EDVAC and all the computers that came later did exactly the same thing. Unlike ENIAC, they cannot be rewired to be different computers: they implement the 'fetch-execute cycle', designed for, and only useful for, emulating different computers. When we program a computer, we are actually designing a new computer and simply telling the fetch-execute cycle how it should work.

This is a rather esoteric distinction that can be difficult to wrap your head around. Our concept of a computer is of a fixed piece of hardware that accepts programs. We are not used to thinking of a program as a recipe for creating a new computer. However, it is important to appreciate this mathematical grounding of computers in order to understand the limits and the possibilities of artificial intelligence. If we say that the brain is a computer – and, by this definition, it almost definitely is – then we can be certain that we can program a computer to do the same things a brain does. Similarly, since any machine that we can design can be described by mathematics, no matter how different from a computer such a device appears to be, it can be emulated by a computer.

Computers are everywhere

You will find a computer in almost every electronic device, often simply because they are cheaper than any other option. A basic toaster doesn't need a computer but having that single component instead of a dozen others that together perform the same function reduces the production cost.

Such computers come in a wide range of speeds and sizes, but they are all fundamentally capable of doing the same things. The memory of the computer in your toaster may be inadequate to hold a spreadsheet program and it doesn't have a screen to display it on nor a keyboard or a mouse for you to interact with it, but those are only physical limitations. If you were to attach more memory and the right peripherals to it, it would be possible to use it to run any program you wanted.[16]

Of course in this book we have no particular interest in toasters. But what about robots? They are only electronic devices with particular peripherals, such as arms or wheels that enable them to interact with their environment.

Like the toaster, the computers they contain are capable of running the same programs as any other computer. A program that is used in a data centre to distinguish pictures of cats from pictures of dogs may be used to take the images from a robot's camera and recognize objects in its environment.

Computer languages

In the fetch-execute cycle, instructions are fetched from memory in sequence and then executed. The set of instructions that the computer understands determines how efficiently it can be programmed. All computers can do the same work but what one can do in a single instruction, another may require several instructions to carry out. A normal desktop PC has

---

16 In practice, most such computers are able to be programmed only once, in the factory. This is to keep secret the program they run and to reduce the customer support costs that would accrue if everyone was reprogramming them. They are also much slower than a desktop PC and would be slower still when most of their memory was in an external peripheral. However, many devices increasingly have the capability to be upgraded by plugging a cable in and it is a safe bet that for any such device, someone somewhere has learned how to install his or her own software into it instead of the manufacturer-supplied program.

hundreds of different instructions available, including some that are useful for complex mathematics or graphics work. But it is possible to create a computer with only one.[17]

The instructions a computer understands make up a language in the same way a set of words makes a language. This is called machine-code. It's numerical, complex and difficult for a human to write in.

The SSEM, EDVAC and most of the computers that came later store their program in the same memory they use for the data that the program operates on. This means that there can be programs that write and modify other programs. With the computer's help we can design languages that are more expressive and graceful, and instruct the computer to translate them into the language that the fetch-execute cycle understands.

There are many computer languages and several of them are designed for niche applications. Some languages are good for manipulating text and others handle structured data efficiently or implement mathematical concepts concisely. Most, but by no means all, are composed of rules and calculations, which is how most people understand computers.

---

17 One such computer has the single instruction 'subtract, and jump if negative'. It takes three instructions just to add two numbers together but it can do anything that any other computer can do.

Modelling

Computer scientists often talk about building a model of some process or object. They don't mean that they will get out cardboard and balsa wood and make a replica of it. The term 'model' is mathematical jargon for writing out all the equations for how this thing works and calculating them all so it can be experimented on without having actually to exist. Since computers are extremey fast, experiments such as these can give us answers more quickly than a real-life experiment could.

In some circumstances it might be unethical or impractical to conduct the experiment in real life. Climate change is an example of this. We don't have any spare Earths nor the time required to experiment on them. Computer models can be a very simple series of equations or very complex, depending on the sort of information we are looking for.

Suppose we wanted to model the physics of how a rubber ball behaves. In an ideal world, a dropped ball always bounces to a certain fraction of the height from which it was dropped. If we drop it from 1 metre (40 inches) it might bounce up to 0.5 metres (20 inches). Then it will bounce again and this time only get to 0.25 metres (10 inches) and then 0.125 m (5 inches) and so on. The time it takes to bounce is simply derived from the physics for a falling object. That's two very simple equations and two numbers to give us the height of each bounce and the time they take.[18] It would be a trivial task to program such a model on a computer. However, it is not very accurate; the amount that the ball rises on each bounce depends not only on the ball but also on the surface on which it is bouncing. It also loses energy to friction on each bounce, both during the bounce and from air resistance. Adding those factors into the model would require a significant amount of research and knowledge of physics but it would not be an insurmountable task.

Now suppose that we are trying to calculate the path of a tennis ball as it is struck by a racquet and bounces on the court. We would have to take into account several different and complex surfaces that the ball will contact at varying angles – and the ball will be spinning, too. Each bounce heats up the air inside the ball and changes its properties. This would be a significantly difficult model to build.

Finally, suppose we were designing some odd weapon that fired rubber balls at great velocity at a target, so fast that they shattered on impact. Now we might have to model the substance that the ball is made of and track individual fragments as they flew away. We might even have to simulate each individual atom in the ball before we have a model accurate enough for

---

18 An ideal ball always bounces an infinite number of times before it comes to rest but since the time each bounce takes is also reducing it completes these infinite bounces in a finite time. Of course, ideal balls do not exist but if one takes a steel ball bearing and drops it onto a very hard surface such as concrete or stone, one can hear the bounces turn from a rhythmical tap into an audible tone with an accelerating rising pitch. It sounds like 'zip'.

our purposes. Such a model would run slowly on the computers we presently have but it would be perfectly possible to create it; we know how physics and chemistry work.

Artificial intelligence is, at its most basic and ambitious, an attempt to create a computer model of the human brain. A perfect model would be nice, but something less accurate will probably be effective. In the following chapters we will discuss various methods that have been used to try to produce such a model.

Some of them have produced useful products but proved too simplistic for our purposes. Others show promise. Some try to simulate the operation of logic and reason, others attempt to simulate brain cells. Most researchers believe that the answer is to be found somewhere around these levels of detail. However, if it is necessary to model the individual cells in greater detail there is nothing fundamentally impossible about doing so, although we may have to wait another decade or so for our computers to be powerful enough to run the model at a decent speed.

CHAPTER 4

The History of Artificial Intelligence

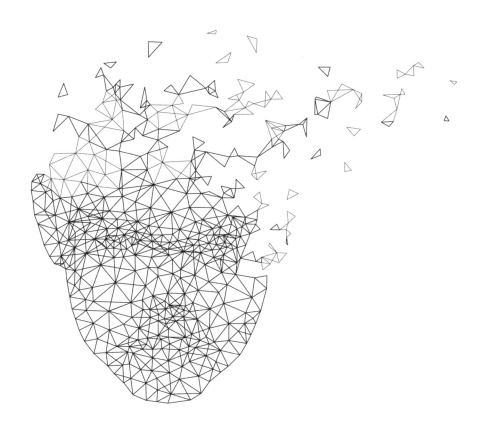

The invention of the computer was the last piece of the puzzle that allowed research into artificial intelligence to begin in earnest. However, some progress had been made previously. Artificial neurons were described by Warren S. McCulloch and Walter Pitts in 1943,[19] when they proved that a Turing-complete machine could be built from them. This was a purely theoretical machine; it would need many vacuum tubes to create each artificial neuron, whereas it only requires a few to construct the logic gates[20] of which computers are composed.

In 1950, Alan Turing wrote a paper entitled 'Computing Machinery and Intelligence',[21] in which he pointed out the difficulties of defining intelligence. He proposed that a computer that could converse indistinguishably from a human could be described, at least in informal speech, as thinking. This assessment – whether a computer could converse like a human – became known as the Turing Test. We shall consider it in detail later.

Shortly after their development, computers were used for the first experiments in artificial intelligence. These were small and slow machines. The Manchester Mark I (of which the SSEM

19 W.S. McCulloch and W. Pitts, 'A Logical Calculus of Ideas Immanent in Nervous Activity', *Bulletin of Mathematical Biophysics*, 5 (1943): 115–33.
20 Logic gates are electronic circuits consisting of one or more inputs and one output, creating a specific logic relationship between input and output.
21 Cited in footnote 13.

was a prototype) had a memory of only 640 bytes and a clock speed of 555Hz. (In comparison a modern desktop PC may have a memory of 4 billion bytes and a clock speed of 3 billion Hz.) This meant that the problems selected for them had to be carefully chosen. For the first decade artificial intelligence programs were concerned with basic applications. They would be the building blocks of research from then on, and particularly with searching.

The Logic Theory machine,[22] described in 1956, attempted to prove mathematical theorems by starting with five axioms and then deducing every theorem between there and the goal. Such problems are like mazes. You can assume that you will make the best progress by moving in the general direction of the goal, but in practice that will not always lead to success. The Logic Theory machine failed to solve more complex problems for this reason. It selected equations that seemed closer to the goal and discarded the ones that seemed to move it further away. However it often ended up discarding the very equations that it needed to use.

Also in 1956, John McCarthy of Dartmouth College, Marvin Minsky of Harvard University, Nathaniel Rochester of IBM Corporation and Claude Shannon of the Bell Telephone Laboratories organized the Dartmouth Summer Research Project on Artificial Intelligence at Dartmouth College in

22 A. Newell and H.A. Simon, 'The Logic Theory Machine: A Complex Information Processing System', Technical Report P-868 (1956), The Rand Corporation, accessed 8 January, 2016, http://shelf1.library.cmu.edu/IMLS/MindModels/logictheorymachine.pdf

Hanover, New Hampshire. This was a two-month workshop on AI that drew together the leading researchers in the field and was a seminal event – not least because the term 'artificial intelligence' was invented for the title of the project.

By 1959, American computing pioneer Arthur Samuel's Checkers program[23] was using a more pragmatic approach than the Logic Theory machine. The Checkers program involved a process similar to the genetic algorithms that were to be devised a decade or more later: the program learned over time how to score each board position by playing against itself in a series of games; by comparing the board positions that would follow each proposed move, it could avoid bad moves and choose good moves.

Saint ... Eliza

In 1961, American mathematician James R. Slagle wrote a program called SAINT, which was able to solve calculus problems about as well as a freshman college student – a first-year undergraduate. Although it was focused on the esoteric field of calculus it was really another attempt to solve the search problem. It worked not by searching all possibilities for the solution, but by decomposing the problem into parts that could be solved more easily.

In 1964, American PhD student Danny Bobrow showed that

23 A.L. Samuel, 'Some Studies in Machine Learning Using the Game of Checkers', *IBM Journal on Research and Development*, 3 (3) (1959): 210–29.

computers could be programmed to understand natural language (in this case, English) in sufficient depth that they could be asked to solve simple algebraic equations.[24] A year later German-born computer scientist Joseph Weizenbaum's ELIZA program conversed with its user competently enough that some were convinced it was a real person.

The year 1966 saw the inaugural Machine Intelligence workshop at Edinburgh in the UK. This was the first of a series of annual conferences. However, in the same year the publication of a damning report on the state of machine translation (translating one human language to another) greatly reduced available funding for natural language research for several years. This was to be a frequent event as progress in artificial intelligence has always proved to be slower than its more vocal proponents predict.

The first successful expert system[25] was demonstrated in 1967. Called DENDRAL,[26] it aided chemists analyzing data from mass spectroscopy (an analytical chemistry technique that helps identify the amount and type of chemicals present in a sample

---

24 For example, 'If Anne makes twice as much money in seven days as Brian makes in three days, and Brian makes £100 in one day, how much money does Anne make in 30 days?' See Daniel G. Bobrow, 'Natural Language Input for a Computer Problem Solving System', *MIT Artificial Intelligence Lab Publications, AI Technical Reports*, 1 March, 1964, accessed 29 January, 2016, http://hdl.handle.net/1721.1/5922

25 See page 66, 'Expert Systems'

26 Robert K. Lindsay, Bruce G. Buchanan, E.A. Feigenbaum and Joshua Lederberg (1993). 'DENDRAL: A Case Study of the First Expert System for Scientific Hypothesis Formation', *Artificial Intelligence* 61, 209–61, accessed 8 January, 2016, http://profiles.nlm.nih.gov/BB/A/B/O/M/

by measuring the light it emits when heated) to identify individual compounds.

In 1968, Richard Greenblatt, a programmer at the Massachusetts Institute of Technology (MIT) created a program that played chess well enough to achieve a class-C rating in tournament play – about as well as a committed member of a chess club.

The year 1969 saw the first International Joint Conference on Artificial Intelligence (IJCAI) at Stanford University, California. In the same year, Marvin Minsky and Seymour Papert, two MIT professors, published a book called *Perceptrons* (another name for artificial neurons), which pointed out some previously unforeseen weaknesses in them. This probably caused a significant reduction in research for a decade or two after.

In 1970 Seppo Linnainmaa published a method for doing the massive differentiations that are necessary for back propagation in deep neural networks[27] but this wouldn't be applied to such networks for a decade and was only universally accepted by 2010.

SHRDLU was the subject of American student Terry Winograd's PhD thesis at MIT in 1971. It used an imaginary robotic arm to move imaginary blocks around. SHRDLU accepted commands in natural English and replied similarly. It could formulate a plan to reach its goal. For example, if it needed to put the blue block on the red block but the yellow block was already there, it would know it was necessary to remove the yellow block first. It understood words such as 'it' from the previous context. One could say

27 Linnainmaa. The representation of the cumulative rounding error of an algorithm as a Taylor expansion of the local rounding errors. Master's Thesis (in Finnish), Univ. Helsinki, 1970.

'pick up the red block' and then 'put it on the blue block'. It also remembered all of its actions and could describe them and why they were necessary when it was asked.

Freddy

The Assembly Robotics Group at the University of Edinburgh built Freddy in 1973. It used binocular vision to identify parts of a model and then built the model from the parts, taking about 16 hours to do so. The 1973 Lighthill Report, however, gave a negative verdict on the progress of AI research in the UK, which resulted in a radical reduction in government funding.

The next year Paul Werbos, an American PhD student at Harvard University, described a method of allowing artificial neural networks to learn. By the mid-1980s this was widely used and ended the period of disuse that had begun in 1969.

In 1975, Canadian-born computer scientist and doctor Ted Shortliffe's PhD dissertation at Stanford University described MYCIN. Borrowing ideas from DENDRAL, it advised doctors on medical diagnosis. Unfortunately it was little used since it took longer to describe the patient's symptoms than it would generally take for the doctor to come to the same decision. It did, however, strongly influence many future expert systems that were to become successful commercial products by the mid-1980s. Also in 1975, Marvin Minsky published a widely read article on frames as a method of representing knowledge.

Hans Moravac built the Standford Cart in 1979. This became

Deep Blue, the computer that beat a chess Grand Master, 1977.

the first autonomous vehicle capable of crossing a room full of obstructions and circumnavigating the AI laboratory. The first National Conference of the American Association for Artificial Intelligence was held in 1980. In 1986 Ernst Dickmanns's team at Bundeswehr University, Germany, built autonomous cars that drove at 90 kilometre/hour (55 miles/hour) on empty roads.

In 1987, Marvin Minsky published a paper describing the mind as a group of co-operating agents, and Rodney Brooks developed the subsumption architecture for robots that operated in much the same manner.

In the Gulf War of 1991, the DART (Dynamic Analysis and Replanning Tool) program was used to plan resource allocations in the war zone and was said to have paid back investment by the US government's Defense Advanced Research Project Agency (DARPA)[28] in the previous 30 years of funding artificial intelligence research.

In 1994, two robot cars with safety drivers and passengers drove more than 1,000 kilometres (620 miles) on busy Paris streets – and later from Munich to Copenhagen. The safety driver approved manoeuvres, such as passing other cars, and took over control completely for such tricky situations as road works. In the same year, the computer program Chinook forced the world draughts (checkers) champion to resign and beat the second-ranked player. Three years later, Deep Blue beat the

---

28 The Defense Advanced Research Projects Agency is an agency of the US Department of Defense tasked with supporting research that will aid the country's military. The Internet was originally one of its projects.

world chess champion and Logistello defeated the world Othello champion 6-0.

Hochreiter and Schmidhuber invented the Long Short-term Memory (LSTM)[29] as a variation of the usual perception in 1997. By giving the perceptron a degree of memory, it allowed networks to handle sequential inputs (such as music or text) with smaller networks and less training.

Tiger Electronics introduced Furby to the market in 1998 as the first AI to be sold into a domestic environment. A year later Sony released AIBO.

Cynthea Breazeal at MIT published her dissertation in 2000 describing Kismet, a robot with a face that expressed emotions.

iRobot introduced the Roomba, an autonomous vacuum cleaner in 2002.

The US government's National Aeronautics and Space Administration (NASA)'s rovers 'Spirit' and 'Opportunity' landed on Mars in 2004. Due to the long delay suffered by radio signals they were required to operate autonomously with only general commands issued from Earth. The technology has improved since. The rover Perseverance, which touched down in 2022, can now take stereo photographs fast enough, and has the processing power, to be able to continue to plan its route while it is driving. Previous rovers had to stop to plan the next section of the drive.

By 2005, technology that tracks web and media activity

29 Hochreiter, S., & Schmidhuber, J. (1997). Long short-term memory. Neural Computation, 9(8), 1735–1780. https://doi.org/10.1162/neco.1997.9.8.1735

allowed companies to recommend products that individual customers would likely have an interest in. IBM's Watson computer beat Brad Rutter and Ken Jennings, champions on the US TV show *Jeopardy!* in 2011.

In 2012, the neural network AlexNet[30] proved the value of Convolutional Neural Networks and GPU-based learning. The Graphic Processing Unit (GPU) in a PC needs to have the ability to make many calculations in order to portray perspective and special effects in 3D graphics. That is precisely what is needed to train neural networks. More recently GPUs have been developed specifically for deep-learning use with fewer graphic-specific processors and more vector-calculating ones. In 2018 Google released Tensorflow. This, and other tools and device drivers, allow anyone to design neural networks that are trained using whatever GPU is available.

By the middle of 2015, the fleet of Google self-driving cars had driven more than 1.5 million kilometres (9 million miles) and only been involved in 14 minor accidents, none of which were the fault of the car. There have been accidents since that were the fault of the car, but the number is small. Google predicted that the technology would become available to the public in 2020. They have since pulled back from this to concentrate on automatic taxis. In 2016 Google spun the technology off as a start-up company called Waymo. They have driverless taxis operating in several US cities. Two problems prevent wider

30 Krizhevsky, Alex; Sutskever, Ilya; Hinton, Geoffrey E. (2017-05-24). "ImageNet classification with deep convolutional neural networks". Communications of the ACM. 60 (6): 84–90. doi:10.1145/3065386. ISSN 0001-0782. S2CID 195908774

adoption. Firstly there are regulatory issues – cars have to have a driver by law. In addition, cars have to have highly detailed maps in order to keep track of their position. These maps will continually change as the road infrastructure develops.

CHAPTER 5

Do As I Say, Not As I Do

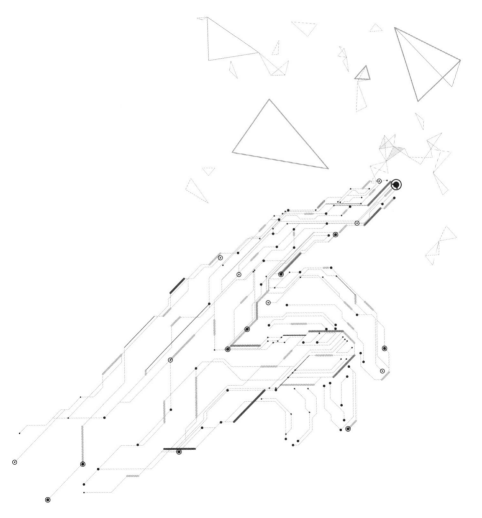

The first researchers to attempt to create artificial intelligence assumed that all you needed were sufficient rules. It was clear from the outset that to create a complete human-like mind would entail writing a lot of rules, probably more than their computers could handle, so they started small. Since it was obvious that only a human could play games like chess, this was one of the first problems that they tackled.

Winning strategies

The easiest of games that computers can be programmed to play are those that have winning strategies. In the game 21, play starts when the first player says '1' and alternates between the players with each saying a number that is 1, 2 or 3 higher than the last. No player can say a number higher than 21 and the player who says '21' loses the game. A game might go as follows:

> Alice: 1
> Bob: 3
> Alice: 6
> Bob: 9
> Alice: 11
> Bob: 14
> Alice: 17

Bob: 19

Alice: 20

Bob: 21. He loses the game.

As we can see from this example, the winning strategy is to be sure that you are the player that makes the move to 20 because only then is your opponent forced into making the losing move. Therefore your previous move must ensure you have a chance to move to 20 and your opponent does not. So your move must be below 17. However, your subsequent addition plus your opponent's addition must add up to 20. You cannot move more than 3 and your opponent might only move 1. Therefore the lowest move you can make is 16. It follows that the player that makes the move to 16 will win, and we can repeat the same argument again and prove that 12, 8 and 4 are also winning moves.

A computer could be programmed easily to play this game. It only needs to move to a multiple of 4 if it is allowed, and otherwise to make a random move.

Such programs are certainly using the same reasoning that a human uses but they are not very interesting nor do they teach us much about intelligence.

Min-Max

If there is no winning strategy, the computer can search for the best move it can make. Let's assume its opponent has said '17'. It can consider each of its possible moves – 18, 19 or 20 – and decide which one is best. For each one it has to investigate its opponent's subsequent moves, and then its own next move and so on. It starts with 18, to which its opponent can reply 19, 20 or 21. Obviously 21 would be good but in the other cases it would have to make another move and those will have to be looked at in turn and so on. It will have to check all these possibilities (the computer's moves are underlined):

18, 19, 20, 21
18, 19, 21
18, 20, 21
18, 21
19, 20, 21
19, 21
20, 21

We have to assume that our opponent will use its strongest move and we hope that we will, too. So when we consider each of our moves we will discard the ones with least chance of us winning, but when we consider each of our opponent's moves we will discard the ones with the least chance of us losing. This is called the Min-Max strategy – we choose the maximum advantage when choosing our moves, and the minimum advantage when selecting our opponent's moves. Applying it to the moves listed above, we are left with:

18, 20, 21
19, 20, 21
20, 21

Moving to 18 or 19 would lead to our defeat because in both cases our opponent can move to 20 and force a win. If we want to win our only possible move is 20. Of course, we knew that already because we know there is a winning strategy.

Even here, on what will be our last move, there are still seven possible games to investigate, with a total of 14 different moves. Earlier in the game there will be even more. In fact, from the start there are 121,415 games and 266,078 moves that have to be considered. Those are large numbers for a person to think about but a computer can handle them with ease. In such a simple game there are obvious techniques we can use to reduce the effort. For example, once we have investigated a move to 15 we can remember the results thereafter.

The number of possible games and moves gets much bigger in more complex games. Chess is estimated to have around 1,000 million, million, million, million, million, million, million possible board positions in any one game. (Mathematicians represent such large numbers in exponential form. This one would be 10^{45}, which you can read as 1 with 45 zeros after it.) Even if, like Deep Blue, our computer could evaluate 200 million positions per second, it would still take 2 million, million, million, million (2×10^{24}) years to make the first move, which is unfortunate because the Earth will not last that long. Any program that takes less time must therefore only look ahead a limited number of moves and evaluate the resulting board positions strategically. There are an average of 30 moves that can be made at any given time

Joseph Weizenbaum, author of the ELIZA program.

in a game of chess, so looking at only two moves for each player involves 810,000 board positions. Three moves would be 729,000,000 board positions, which would take a computer a significant time but would still be feasible. Unfortunately, a player who looks only three moves ahead plays poor chess. Instead of looking at all of those positions and being limited to only seeing three moves ahead, there are optimizations that can be made. If many pieces are being taken, then the program can look ahead further to see how the exchange pans out. Other possible sequences can be disregarded early if they seem to be uninteresting.

In the last decades of the 20th century it was thought that aggressive pruning of unpromising sequences would allow in-depth evaluation of the stronger moves. In fact it turned out that evaluating the moves sufficiently accurately to make those optimizations took longer than just evaluating all the moves. Modern programs tend to be only lightly optimized, which is a little disappointing from an artificial intelligence point of view, since strong human players tend to consider only around 40 board positions per move; they know from experience which moves are worth considering. Speaking from experience, as a very poor player, I certainly find evaluating moves and formulating strategy the hardest part of chess, which is the easiest part to program. While I don't decide which moves are interesting nearly as well as a strong player, I probably ignore well over half of the available moves at any time (mostly correctly), and that is the bit that is difficult to program.

Natural language

Another topic that was researched early on in the development of artificial intelligence was natural language conversation. Humans learn how to speak in their first couple of years and only move on to reading and writing later. Computers find understanding speech formidably difficult but text is simple. Even so, almost no existing conversation program could be said to understand what the user is saying in any meaningful way. A few of the more advanced ones make some attempt to decide which are the nouns, verbs and so forth in a sentence but most of them don't even do that.

A conversation with Eliza

One of the first conversation programs was ELIZA, which was written to explore how people might attribute a personality to a computer program. ELIZA played the part of a psychotherapist. Here is a representative excerpt of a conversation with a recreation of the original program:[31]

'Hello, Doctor.'

'How do you do? What brings you to see me?'

'I can't sleep.'

'Why do you say you cannot sleep?'

31 Although the original paper described the operation of the program in detail, it did not include the program itself. This conversation was held with the doctor program in Gnu Emacs, which appears to be approximately equivalent to the original. See Gnu Operating System, accessed 8 January, 2016, http://www.gnu.org/software/emacs/

'I lie in bed staring at the ceiling.'

'Is it because of your plans that you say you lie in bed staring at the ceiling?'

'I don't have any plans.'

'Maybe your life has something to do with this.'

'My life is good.'

'What makes you believe your life is good?'

'I make more money than my father ever earned.'

'Tell me something about your family.'

Joseph Weizenbaum, the program's author, reported that people using it quickly formed emotional attachments to it, treating it as a real psychotherapist. Some of them refused to believe that they were not talking to a real person. When he proposed adding a facility to store the conversations, in order to examine them later, Weizenbaum was accused of trying to spy on people's intimate secrets. This is all the more surprising when ELIZA could only have been said to have understood at most two words of anything the user typed in. One of the rules it follows is for a sentence that begins 'I': all it does then is to spit the same sentence out again with the pronouns changed and a random bit at the beginning. There are two examples of this above. Here is another one:

'I fjklds fjdklsjf.'

'Do you really think you fjklds fjdklsjf?'

Modern chatbots, as these programs have become known, are a little more sophisticated than this early example. They can match words that occur close to each other in a sentence and they can store some information for later use. You can tell them

'My car is blue,' and they will understand that something called a 'car' is a colour 'blue'. They can also be connected to a database and use that as an additional source of knowledge. If they were on a bank's website, they could tell you your account balance.

Just like the chess programs, these chat programs don't look much like intelligence. At most they could be said to offer an insight into a human's propensity to anthropomorphize the most basic of machines, which was Weizenbaum's conclusion.

Hard to understand

Other people tried to write similar programs that parsed the user's input into nouns, verbs and so on. But they immediately found that the task was much harder than they had assumed. In order to converse, a computer needs to understand a huge amount about the world. Take this sentence:

'Time flies like an arrow.'

Its meaning is clear and simple to us but fraught with uncertainty for a computer. There are four different ways it can be parsed, all meaning different things. If the others are not apparent, here are some alternative versions of the same sentence form:

'A dart flies like an arrow.' (The verb is "flies".)

'Fruit flies like a banana.' (The verb is "like".)

'Time marathons like a grand prix.' (The verb is "time".)

In order for the computer to know which meaning is correct, it would need to know that time is not a physical object, that there is no such organism as a time fly and that nobody is particularly interested in timing flies. While the first of these might make it into a database of common sense, it is unlikely that any programmer would think to include the last. Even if the structure of a sentence is obvious, its meaning still needs a lot of background knowledge. It is straightforward to take a sentence such as, 'The cat stared at the mouse', and deduce that in a past instant, something called a cat performed an action known as staring at an object called a mouse, but that knowledge is of little use unless one knows what a cat and mouse are and what is involved in staring. A computer program would have to be highly complex and its database very comprehensive before it could be said to reproduce the what-happens-next tension the sentence evokes in a human reader.

Such programs have their place in restricted worlds, where their database does not have to be so big. Computer adventure games always used to be driven by the user typing text such as 'go north', and this evolved so far as to allow instructions such as 'say to Jack "give sword to Julie"'. Then came the point and click graphical games and text became too slow to use. Many games now contain conversations with people but the player is limited to choosing topics of conversation from a menu. This would be an ideal situation in which to use natural language parsing; the world is restricted, the computer is able to know everything about it and the gaming machines are powerful enough to support it – if the graphics developers don't hog the power themselves. Text input may still be too slow for most people to use, but speech input is getting better all the time.

Expert systems

Another line of enquiry was the expert system. These allow the user to enter a list of data and the system deduces facts from that data. An example would be a medical diagnostician: the doctor enters all the symptoms that the patient displays and the computer diagnoses which disease is present. Unfortunately, the early attempts to create such systems failed for the same reasons the others did – knowledge. Medical experts are not able to regurgitate every fact they know in a complete and logical pattern, and adding facts to an existing system involves rewriting part of the program. What was required was a way to represent the medical facts separately from the program itself, just as the chatbots needed a world database.

CHAPTER 6

Frames, Knowledge and Learning

Let's invent an expert system for dealing with household problems. First we talk to a lot of experts and we compile a long list of rules, such as:

IF there is a power cut THEN all lights and all the appliances don't work

IF the fuse has blown THEN all lights don't work OR all the appliances don't work

IF a bulb has failed THEN a light doesn't work

IF an appliance has failed THEN an appliance doesn't work

WHEN there is a power cut YOU SHOULD wait

WHEN the fuse has blown YOU SHOULD mend the fuse

WHEN a bulb has failed YOU SHOULD change the bulb

WHEN an appliance has failed YOU SHOULD get the appliance repaired.

We will also need to add to this some common sense rules:

IF all the lights don't work THEN a light doesn't work

IF all the appliances don't work THEN an appliance doesn't work

IF all the lights and all the appliances don't work THEN all the lights don't work

IF all the lights and all the appliances don't work
THEN all the appliances don't work.

The first expert systems took this sort of data and made it an integral part of a program, which would end up saying something like:

'If the problem is a light doesn't work, then ask whether all the lights don't work. If the other lights are OK then tell the user to change the bulb. Otherwise ask if the appliances work. If the appliances are not working, then tell the user there is a power cut and they should wait. Otherwise tell them to mend the fuse.

'If the problem is an appliance doesn't work, then ask whether all the appliances don't work. If the other appliances are OK, then tell the user to get the failed one repaired. Otherwise ask if the lights work. If the lights are not working, then tell the user there is a power cut and they should wait. Otherwise tell them to mend the fuse.'

This is a perfectly valid way to create such an expert system but it is very inflexible. We cannot ask it, 'What are the symptoms of a power cut?' nor can we easily add knowledge to it. Let's say our experts come back to us the day after the system is finished and say that they forgot something. When we grill them further we find the following new rules:

IF the earth leakage breaker has tripped THEN all
lights and all the appliances don't work

IF there is a power cut THEN the other houses in the
street are dark

WHEN the earth leakage breaker has tripped YOU
SHOULD reset the breaker.

Now we need to go back to our program and find the paragraphs that correspond to lights and appliances not working and insert new instructions to deal with the earth leakage breaker in just the right places. Making those changes is complex and error-prone.

Instead, we can make the rules separate from the program and write the program to use the rules to search for a recommendation. It will do this by making and testing hypotheses just as a human would. If we tell it the light doesn't work it will search for all the reasons why that might happen: a bulb has failed or all the lights don't work. We can check the latter by asking the user if the other lights work. When we hear that they do, we can conclude that the bulb has failed and suggest that the user changes it. If we have to change some rules, we can do that without touching the program at all. In fact, the same program could be used with an entirely different set of rules, maybe to diagnose faults on a car or decide whether to offer a bank customer a loan.

Frames

Writing out all the rules like that works well enough for logical problems with yes and no answers. When the problem gets more complex, we need something more flexible. If we want our chatbot to be able to engage in small talk, we need to give it a lot of knowledge about the world. It needs to know such things as that the sky is blue and that lemon goes with tea but orange doesn't. We do that with frames. Every concept that the program knows about has a frame and in the frame are any number of individual relationships. We might record that Sue is 27-years-old and works in a hospital.

As we have seen, before the chatbot is able to continue any conversation there is a lot we have to teach it, but it can also learn other things during the conversation. While it was talking to Sue it might discover that her husband's name was Jack. It could then create a new frame for Jack and put a relationship into both of the frames to show that they were married. The program will know that Jack must be human, so it can link it to the frame for humans. Now it knows that Jack has two arms and two legs, because all humans do. Of course, Jack might really be an amputee and the program is setting itself up for an embarrassing faux pas; but that is precisely the sort of mistake a human might make in the same situation. Once it has apologized, it can make a note in Jack's frame that although a human generally has two legs, Jack only has one. The longer the program converses, the more it will learn. It takes a human child a decade or maybe

Watson, the computer that played Jeopardy!

two to achieve fluency in conversation but a computer can read much faster than any human and the Internet has as much knowledge as it might need.

Elementary, my dear

When in 2011 the IBM computer Watson beat two human champions on the TV quiz show *Jeopardy!* it had not only to understand the questions posed in natural English but also to search a database generated from 2 million pages of natural English in order to find the answer. Once it understood the question it searched its database and found a number of possible answers. Each of those answers was checked in hundreds of different ways to ensure it was correct and relevant.

Watson sorted the answers that passed scrutiny according to their likelihood of being right, based on what it had learned over many hours of practise using old questions from the show. This is not so dissimilar to the way a chess program tests many different possible moves, but it is being done using real world and imperfect data rather than an abstract game and perfect data.

IBM is now using the Watson technology in products for customer relations, healthcare and finance. Currently it is only used by doctors and call-centre chat-bots.

Frames are very useful for arranging and storing knowledge, but they suffer from the same difficulties that plagued chess programs; to represent enough knowledge to allow a computer to converse freely on any subject there would be more frames than can be easily searched in a reasonable time. Processor power increases all the time. Watson was the size of a room but modern implementations are about the size of a regular desktop PC. Nevertheless, the human brain is rather a slow processor; signals travel through it at around 120 metres (393 feet) per second, not the speed of light. If we are asked to name a person with red hair, we do not consciously list every person we know and wonder if their hair is red. One cannot help but think that there must be some way to make access to knowledge more efficient.

Watson doesn't converse; it would be less useful if it did. It only understands language so that it can understand questions and reference material. The answers it gives are precise and offered with a measure of how confident Watson is in them. Answering questions precisely is a fairly trivial use of language. I stopped learning French in school because I found it boringly formulaic. When asked 'Where is your aunt's pen?' I only had to rearrange the question and insert the answer. 'My aunt's pen is ...' Of course, if I had stuck to it for another year or two I would have been able to answer 'It was in the study when she was doing the crossword. Have you looked down the side of the chair?'

There may be hope for Watson, though: there is a story that IBM had to stop it referencing the *Urban Dictionary*[32] because it started swearing. Even so, generating natural replies that evoke a consistent personality and respond to the other person's demeanour is a whole new problem.

---

32 The *Urban Dictionary*, http://www.urbandictionary.com/ is a crowd-sourced dictionary of street slang. It is not recommended for those who may be easily offended.

CHAPTER 7

Fuzzy Logic

The normal sort of binary logic used by computers has only two states; a statement is either true or it is false. In the real world, however, situations are rarely so clear-cut. One is not either hungry or not hungry; being a little peckish is not the same as being ravenous. Being a little chilly is far less important than freezing to death. Rules that we write in computer programs can easily get over-complex once we take account of all the gradations in meaning.

An insect has a number of instincts that tell it how to react in various conditions. It might tend to move away from light. That makes it hide under leaves and rocks so predators can't find it easily. On the other hand, it will move towards food, otherwise it will starve. If we were building a robot beetle, we could give it some rules such as:

IF the light is over 50 per cent and food quality is under 50 per cent, THEN move away OTHERWISE move towards.

What happens if the food and the light are in the same place? A well-fed insect should stay safe in the dark, whereas if it is hungry it should risk danger in order to eat. The brighter the light, the more dangerous it is, and the higher quality the food is, the more danger the insect should risk in order to eat it. We could model this with some more rules:

IF hungry and light is over 75 per cent and food quality is under 25 per cent, THEN move away OTHERWISE move towards.

However, such rules do not handle extremes very well. Our robot could starve to death because the light was 76 per cent or the food quality was only 24 per cent, but it would endanger itself more than might be reasonable were the numbers just 1 per cent different. We can add some more rules to take care of the extremes and special cases, but before long the program will become a mess that nobody understands. How can we handle all the variations without adding complexity?

Maybe we are running a dating agency. One of our clients has said she wants tall men but not rich men. One of the men on our books is 1.78 metres (5 feet 8 inches) tall and earns twice the national average salary per year. Should we introduce them? How can we judge what is tall or rich and, worse, how can we score the men in our database in order to find the best match? We can't subtract salary from height any more than we can add apples and oranges.

Dating dilemmas

Fuzzy logic was devised to answer these sorts of questions. In normal logic, the conditions in the rules above are either true or false, 1 or 0. There is either light or there is not, a man is either tall or not tall. In fuzzy logic the truth value of a condition can have any value between 0 and 1. We might say that a man over 2 metres (6 feet 5 inches) high is definitely tall, and a man under 1.7 metres (5 feet 5 inches) is certainly not tall. Then we can say that our 1.78 metre-tall (5 feet 8

A beetle hides in the dark before coming out to feed.

inches) client is maybe 0.55 tall – not definitively tall, but he certainly has some degree of tallness about him. To find the degree to which he is not tall we simply subtract the number from 1. So he is 0.55 tall and 0.45 not-tall.

We might also have a category for shortness and we might decide that a man under 1.6 metres (5 feet 2 inches) was certainly short and someone over 1.75 metres (5 feet 7 inches) was not-short. Notice that the definitions for tall and short overlap. What we are saying is that someone in the middle is to a certain degree tall and to another degree short. Short is not the same as not-tall; there will be different numbers for tall, short, not-tall and not-short.

Similarly we might say he was 0.2 rich, which makes him 0.8 not-rich. Our first client has specified 'tall and not rich' and so we need to calculate '0.55 and 0.8', which we might decide is 0.44.[33] We can sort through all our candidates and select the ones with the highest score to introduce to our client.

Similarly, our insect might have a rule that tells it to move towards the food if it is hungry and the light is not-bright.

33 There is more than one way to calculate AND and OR operations in fuzzy logic. The choice of which one to use is a pragmatic one based on how the numbers need to behave. Here I have chosen to multiply them. Another mathematically purer method would be to take the lowest of the two numbers. However, then the larger number would have no effect on the outcome; a man the same height but only 0.5 not-rich would have the same result as our 0.8 not-rich man.

Problem-solving

These two examples show the types of problems that can be solved with fuzzy logic. Expert systems are built using the expertise of humans. If we are lucky they will give specific rules that can be included in the system. They might say, 'If the temperature is over 95 degrees for two minutes, or 97 degrees for one minute, then the thermostat is broken.' Unfortunately, they are much more likely to say, 'If the temperature is too high for too long, then the thermostat might be broken', and it is up to the programmer to put the specific numbers in. With fuzzy logic we can make rules that say just the same as the expert.

IF temperature IS too high AND time that temperature too high IS too long THEN thermostat IS broken

The program will then assign a value to the proposition that the 'thermostat is broken', somewhere in the range 0 to 1. If the temperature is only a little high and it hasn't been high for very long, the proposition might get a value of 0.1, not very likely. Other rules will probably have higher outcomes. For instance, if another rule determines that the input cooler being broken has a value of 0.95, the program will report that the most likely cause of the fault is the input cooler. The numbers are termed possibilities. They are not probabilities; there is not a 10 per cent chance that the thermostat is broken any more than our value of 0.55 for the tallness of a man is the chance that he is tall. It is merely a measure of how sure we are that he should be considered to be tall. Similarly, we are concluding that we are 10 per cent certain that the thermostat is broken, but 95 per cent certain that the problem is the input cooler.

A more complex expert system might be deciding whether a bank should agree to loan money to a customer. Some of the rules might be:

IF salary IS high AND job security IS high THEN risk
IS low
IF salary IS low OR job security IS low THEN risk IS
medium
IF credit score IS low THEN risk IS high.

This part of the program might decide that the resulting possibilities are:

risk IS low = 0.1
risk IS medium = 0.7
risk IS high = 0.3.

These three figures can be converted into a single number for risk using mathematical procedures too complex to go into here. (It's called de-fuzzification.) However, we can see that the risk is probably a little on the high side of medium.

Another use of fuzzy logic is to control machinery, such as controlling a heating system. The rules in such a case might be:

IF temperature IS high THEN heat IS off
IF temperature IS very low THEN heat IS high

IF temperature IS low AND rise IS slow THEN heat
   IS high
IF temperature IS low AND rise IS rapid THEN heat
   IS medium
IF temperature IS slightly low AND rise IS slow THEN
   heat IS medium
IF temperature IS slightly low AND rise IS rapid
   THEN heat IS off.

When we apply all of those rules we will find the possibilities that the heat should be off, medium or high. Then we convert those into a single number for how to set the heater.

The fuzzy control system takes the state of the equipment and generates control signals to change that state towards the condition that is desired. Fuzzy control systems excel where the equipment is non-linear, when a certain control has different effects depending on the state of the equipment.

A good fit for human logic?

Fuzzy logic is interesting for two reasons. First it works and it is a useful method for converting human expertise into an automated system. The expert systems and control programs that we can build with it can solve problems that are difficult to solve with mathematical or normal logic systems. But secondly it is interesting because it seems to be a good match for the way our minds work. It converts expertise well because experts express themselves in precisely the way they need to in order to feed into a fuzzy logic program. Something about how it expresses the world as overlapping fuzzy categories matches the way we think.

So far we have seen various methods of creating intelligence that depend on the human programmers creating lists of rules in one form or another. This approach works well and such programs are used in many fields but they all depend on those lists of rules. The problem is that we still don't know how a computer can be made to think. That is what those lists of rules are: attempts to build a thinking program from what we understand about the process of thinking. They have proved pretty conclusively that we do not understand the process of thinking nearly well enough. It would be nice if we could do away with those rules and just specify what we wanted our program to do. The next technologies we discuss are attempts to do exactly that.

CHAPTER 8

Subsumption Architecture

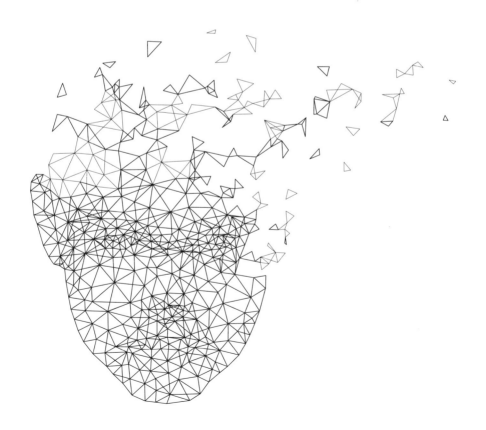

Programming computers in the traditional manner is not easy; the programmer must take into account every situation that the program may encounter and specify how each must be treated. Indeed, more than half the work in creating a program of any size lies in finding those cases that are handled wrongly and modifying the code to correct them.

Over the decades, many tools have been developed to make programming more efficient and reduce the occurrence of errors. While programming is certainly more efficient than it was in 1948 when computers were invented, it is no less error-prone. A programmer will make around the same number of errors per hundred lines of program, no matter which tools are used. It has been said that if someone invented a way to allow computers to be programmed in plain English, we would discover that programmers could not speak plain English. The errors are not only or even mainly in the program itself or the data it uses but in the specification of the task. If a general-purpose artificial intelligence program was to be written using logic, rules and frames, then it would certainly be very big and big programs have a large number of bugs.

The Chinese room

The difficulty of creating a large-scale intelligent system using logic, rules and frames led to doubt as to whether such a thing was ever going to be possible. In 1986, John Searle put forward a thought experiment he called the Chinese room, in order to show that a computer that manipulated symbols could never be said to understand the world, even if it perfectly simulated doing so.

Suppose a man is put into a room with a supply of pencils and paper and a big book of rules. From time to time, slips of paper are passed into the room with 'squiggles' on them. The man looks through the rule book for instructions on how to handle these marks and makes copious notes in the process of doing so. Eventually he produces another slip of paper with other squiggles on it and passes it out of the room. Unbeknown to him, these slips of paper hold questions and answers written in Chinese. The man does not know Chinese and may not even recognize the characters as Chinese at all, and yet the replies coming out of the room are correct answers for the questions going in.

Of course, the man is standing in for a computer, which is doing exactly this: following a set of rules to manipulate symbols. The Chinese Room posits a computer program that displays every sign of being intelligent and yet no part of it could be said to understand the information flowing through it.

Avoiding the use of symbols

According to Searle, this proves that a program that manipulates symbols can never be conscious. This argument has been attacked and defended in several ways since it was originally published and we will return to it later. However, it did have the effect of slowing work on purely logic-based AI in favour of systems that worked without manipulating symbols. One of the more extreme of these attempts was subsumption architecture, which avoids using symbols entirely. Instead of a huge database of frames to model the world, reality is sensed directly.

A subsumption architecture is not a program working on text hidden away in some data centre, it is a physical robot and it uses various devices (sensors) to sense the world and various others (actuators) to manipulate it. Rodney Brookes said, 'The key observation is that the world is its own best model. It is always exactly up to date. It always contains every detail there is to be known. The trick is to sense it appropriately and often enough.'[34]

This is known as situated or embodied[35] AI and it is considered by many to be of prime importance in building an intelligent system that avoids the massive databases that proved so difficult to create. A subsumption architecture is built in layers of independent modules called behaviours. Each of them is a simple program that takes information from sensors and

---

31 Rodney A. Brookes, 'Elephants Don't Play Chess', *Robotics and Autonomous Systems* (1990): 6.

35 The two terms have slightly different meanings. Situated AI is physically placed in a real environment. Embodied AI is provided with a physical body. The former implies that it must interact with a non-ideal environment, the latter that it must do so with non-ideal sensors and actuators. In practice, of course, you can't have one without the other.

issues instructions to actuators. Layers higher up can also inhibit the operation of behaviours lower down.

Allen

The first robot built using these techniques was Allen, which had three layers of behaviours. The bottom layer avoided obstacles, by detecting objects with sonar and moving away from them. By itself it would remain stationary until something moved close to it, whereupon it would run away. The closer the object was, the stronger the impulse to move away from it.

The middle layer modified this behaviour by making the robot move in a random direction every ten seconds. The top layer used the sonar again to look for places that were a long way away and adjusted the robot's path to go there. As an experiment, it was a successful demonstration of the technology, although the robot itself, moving randomly from place to place, did not achieve much.

Herbert

Of rather more use was Herbert,[36] the third robot built using subsumption architecture. It used 24 eight-bit microprocessors to run 40 individual behaviours. Herbert roamed the MIT Artificial Intelligence lab looking for empty drink cans and taking them back to its home base, theoretically for recycling.

---

36 For a full description of Herbert, see Jonathan H. Connell 'A Colony Architecture for an Artificial Creature', *MIT Artificial Intelligence Lab Publications, AI Technical Reports* 1151 (September 1989).

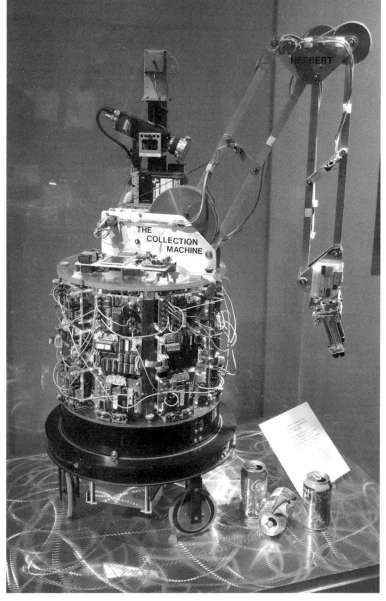

Herbert, the drink-can collecting robot.

Research students, it seems, were prone to leave empty cans lying around. More pragmatically, cans were all the same size and shape, and were invariably encountered in the upright position. This made the cans easier to recognize and manipulate.

Herbert had no memory, and could not plan a path through the laboratory. In addition, none of its behaviours communicated with any of the others; they all took their inputs from sensors and controlled actuators as their outputs. For example, when the arm had been extended so that its fingers were either side of a can, the hand closed, not because the software controlling the arm had completed its operation, but because an infra-red beam between the fingers was interrupted. Likewise, because the hand held a can, the arm retracted.

Herbert was able to react to the world more flexibly than a robot with strict rules and planning might. If, as it was trundling down a hall, someone gave it an empty can, it would grasp it and immediately take it back to its home base. It did not need to abort its search process to do so. The hand closed because the can was there and because the hand was closed on a can its movement became directed toward its home rather than random exploration.

Toto

Although it may seem that without memory a robot could not carry out many useful tasks, researchers developed methods that worked around such limitations. Toto[37] was a robot that wandered around its environment making a map of it, not as a data-structure but as a set of landmarks.

When a landmark was discovered a behaviour was allocated to it. Toto could return to a remembered location simply by activating the behaviour associated with that place. That behaviour repeatedly sent out a message activating the behaviours closest to it and they in turn passed the activation on. Sooner or later the behaviour associated with the robot's current location would be activated. The message that first caused that activation would have come through the smallest number of landmark behaviours and would therefore indicate the optimum path. The robot would move in the direction of the landmark that the activation signal came from. When it got there it would receive a new activation signal and continue in the direction that it indicated. Eventually it would navigate through the shortest path from landmark to landmark to the place it needed to be.

The robot did not detect a landmark as humans might detect it, by recognizing a certain office door, a pot plant or a large printer, but instead by noting aspects of the robot's own behaviour – whether it was following a corridor, a wall or neither. While Toto was only capable of exploring an area and returning to any given part of it on command, a more sophisticated robot

37 Toto is described by M.J. Mataric (1990) 'A Distributed Model for Mobile Robot Environment-Learning and Navigation', *MIT Artificial Intelligence Laboratory Technical Report* AI-TR 1228 (1990).

could associate activities or events with the landmarks and return to them when those conditions were desired. A solar-powered robot could find places where the light was strong and return to them when its batteries were running low. A drinks can collecting robot could remember places where the students were particularly prone to leave cans around.

The subsumption architecture provides compelling explanations for the behaviour of lower animals, such as insects or invertebrates – cockroaches or snails. The programming of a robot that uses the subsumption architecture is fixed. If we want the robot to do something else then we build a different robot. That is not how our brains work; they grow and change as we age and learn. But not all animals have brains as complex as ours. *Caenohabditis elegans* (generally shortened to *C. elegans*) is a nematode worm only 1.2 millimetres (0.04 inches) long that lives in the moisture between soil particles. Its entire central nervous system is composed of only 302 nerve cells.[38] Every individual appears to have exactly the same cells, wired in the same way. It seems that its behaviour is hard-wired; if we want a worm that does something different, we need to find a different sort of worm.

---

38 J.G White, E. Southgate, J.N. Thomson and S. Brenner, 'The Structure of the Nervous System of the Nematode *Caenorhabditis elegans*', *Philosophical Transactions of The Royal Society of London, Series B, Biological Sciences*, vol. 314, no. 1165 (November 12, 1986), 1–340.

Reflexes?

There are many robots for which this degree of intelligence is entirely appropriate. A vacuum cleaner, for example, only needs to be sure to cover the whole floor area in the most efficient manner without being confused by obstacles that might appear and disappear while it operates. But the subsumption architecture may also be useful at the lowest levels of a more intelligent robot, to implement reflexes. We blink when an object approaches our eyes and we snatch our hand away when we touch something painful. Both actions are too quick to have involved conscious thought and in fact reflexes do not necessarily involve the brain; when your doctor taps your knee and watches your leg jerk, the signals only go from the knee up to the spine and back down to the muscles. In particular, if a robot has so much software to run that it thinks relatively slowly, a fast set of reflexes underlying that programming would allow us to build a robot that was both responsive to its environment and intelligent.

This may be the way forward; while the subsumption architecture can successfully reproduce the behaviour of insects, reflexes and so forth, it has not been shown to be able to handle the higher-level reasoning involved with such things as language or high-level learning. It is an important piece of the puzzle, certainly, but it does not seem to be the whole answer.

CHAPTER 9

Neural Networks

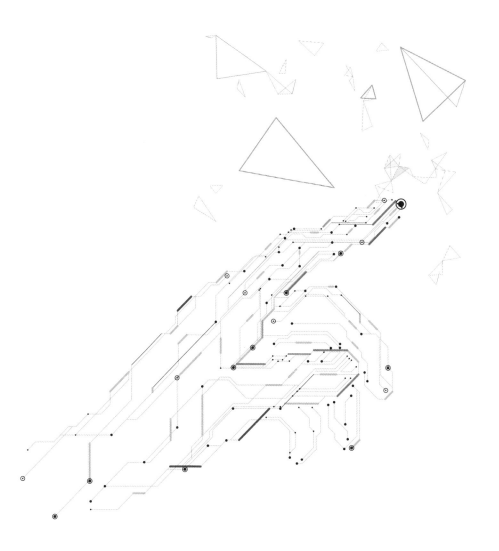

An animal's central nervous system is composed of cells called nerve cells or neurons. Like all cells they have a nucleus containing DNA and a cell membrane that keeps everything else contained. Unlike most other cells, they can be rather large. The nerve cells that receive sense impressions from the toes reach all the way there from the base of the spine. There are neurons in a giraffe's neck that stretch its entire length. Nerve cells generally have three parts: soma, dendrites and axon. The soma is the body of the cell, where the nucleus is. The dendrites are short, branching filaments that receive signals from other nerve cells. The axon is a single long, branching thread that transmits signals to other nerve cells. The connection between the axon of one cell and the dendrite of another is called a synapse.

A nerve cell operates by firing or transmitting a pulse along the axon. The pulse is either there or not there, on or off; it is never stronger or weaker. The signals coming in from other neurons determine how likely a neuron is to fire its own signal. The signals from other cells can make a cell more likely to fire or less likely to fire; or they can alter the effects other signals have. There are neurons that don't fire unless they receive signals and others that fire over and over again unless a signal inhibits them. Some fire more or less frequently depending on the signals they receive. It used to be thought that a nerve cell was a simple device that added together all its signals and fired when the total was over a threshold. However, we are learning that they are capable of somewhat more than this.

Brain-like computers

On average, a human brain contains around 100 billion neurons, each of which connects to an average of 7,000 other neurons. If we make the assumption that the human mind arises from the operation of the brain, and we don't have any better explanation without involving religion,[39] then we can estimate how powerful a computer we need to match a human brain. We will need around one basic operation per synapse and we will need to do them around 1,000 times a second. That's 10^{17} operations per second. The home microcomputer around at the time of writing has a speed of about 10^9 operations per second in each of its four processors – but faster processors do exist. We can reach around 10^{11} operations per second with inexpensive hardware but we would need 1 million such processors to match the human brain. However, computers tend to double in power every 18 months, which means they get 100 times faster every decade. Within the

39 In his 1950 paper, Alan Turing wrote, 'It appears to me that the argument quoted above implies a serious restriction of the omnipotence of the Almighty ... should we not believe that He has freedom to confer a soul on an elephant if He sees fit? We might expect that He would only exercise this power in conjunction with a mutation which provided the elephant with an appropriately improved brain to minister to the needs of this sort. An argument of exactly similar form may be made for the case of machines.' A.M. Turing 'Computing Machinery and Intelligence,' *Mind* 49 (1950): 433–60.

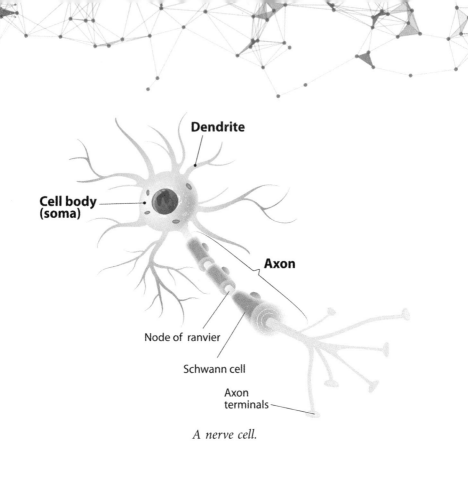

A nerve cell.

next 30 years we can expect to see computers that match the computational power of the human brain.

Of course, having a fast computer is not going to create artificial intelligence instantly. We also need to know how to program it. If the brain is composed of neurons and it is intelligent, maybe we should make our program simulate neurons. After all, this is proven to work.

A neural net is a network of artificial neurons called perceptrons. The artificial neurons that are currently used are simpler than the real ones. They take thousands of inputs, add them together, apply an *activation function*, and produce an output.

Each of the inputs has a configurable weight, so we can set how much effect any given one has on the total. If the weight is negative then it will inhibit firing.

For example, let's say we have a neuron with three inputs, A, B and C, and the activation function outputs 1 if the inputs add up to 2 or more and zero otherwise. Input A is weighted 1, input B is weighted 2 and input C is weighted –1.

If only input A is active, the sum is 1 and the perceptron outputs 0.

If only input B is active then the sum is 2 and perceptron outputs 1.

If input B and input C are both active then the sum is 2 – 1 = 1, and the perceptron outputs 0, but if input A is active as well, the sum is 1 + 2 – 1 = 2 and the output is 1.

These perceptrons can be used to build a computer program but they are more complex than the languages that are already used for that and they don't bring any advantages. Instead we can make large groups of them just like in a brain and allow the weights of all the inputs to change. Then we can train the whole thing to do what we want without having to understand how it is working.

The perceptrons are arranged in at least two layers, and some implementations have as many as 30. Each layer has many perceptrons, maybe a few thousand. So a complete neural network may have 100,000 or more individual perceptrons in it. Each one takes inputs from all of the perceptrons in the layer that comes before it and sends its output to all the perceptrons in the layer that comes after. We use them by injecting signals

An artificial neural network with three layers.

into the first layer and interpreting the outputs from the last layer.

Training a neural net

At first, what comes out of the network is going to be random because we have not instructed it what it needs to do. So we give it a lot of data for which we know the response that the neural net should give. Maybe the problem is to look at pictures of a battlefield and tell us if there are any tanks in the picture. We can take a few thousand pictures with and without tanks and feed them into the first layer of the network. Then we tweak the weights of all the inputs of all of the perceptrons to make the output of the last layer closer to the correct answer. That involves complex mathematics but it can be automated. We repeat this process over and over again, showing it each training image hundreds of times. Gradually the errors reduce further and further until it is responding correctly every time. Once the network is trained, we can give it new pictures and, if we have chosen the training data carefully and run it through enough cycles, it will reliably tell us whether or not there is a tank in the picture.

The main problem with neural nets is that we don't know how they are reaching their conclusions, and therefore we don't know if they are really looking for what we want them to look for. If all the pictures with tanks in were taken on a sunny day and all of the pictures without tanks were taken in the rain, the neural net will probably just tell us whether we need an umbrella or not.

Doing it fast

Neural networks require a vast number of calculations, especially when they are being trained. If two consecutive layers each have a thousand perceptrons in, then there are a million multiplications and additions to be done, and then a thousand more or less complex calculations to determine the output. Modern PCs can do maths very fast. The rather old one I am using now can do 800 million of those multiplications per second. It's fast enough to calculate a single result from a neural network in a reasonable amount of time but it's nowhere near fast enough to do that maybe a thousand times to sample all of the data examples, back-calculate all of the weight changes that are required and do all of that maybe a thousand times to train the network.

A modern gaming PC comes with a graphics card that also has to do a lot of calculations very fast. Gamers want their games to have high-resolution realistic 3D scenery and to create a new frame sixty or more times every second. They need to 'transform' large numbers of 3D coordinates to move models around a scene or to view it from different angles. To do that they have vector processors, which are processors designed to do calculations on lists of numbers all at the same time, rather than one by one. That is precisely the same sort of thing that we need to do with neural networks. As a result, we can train our networks using the power of our graphics cards. The graphics card manufacturers have seen this and created even more powerful cards specifically designed for AI work. Modern neural networks are designed and built with vector processors in mind. They are not so much models of the neurons in a brain, but bundles of calculation that can be done simultaneously.

Why use a neural net?

Because neural nets don't need us to tell them how to get the answer, we can use them even when we don't know how to do what they need to do. Recognizing objects in pictures is one such example. Another might be predicting how the stock market is going to move. So long as there is a large amount of good-quality training data available, a neural net can be programmed to do the job.

Even though artificial neurons are simplified models of real nerve cells, there are some interesting hints that neural nets work the same way the brain does. Scans of the brain show certain areas are sensitive to edges between light and dark that are moving up, down, left or right. Google[40] has neural nets that are trained to recognize objects – so their users can ask to admire pictures of cats. These nets have around 30 layers but Google has shown that the first few layers analyze the picture by looking for edges between objects. They were not programmed to do that; the behaviour emerged just by training the net as a whole.

Neural networks are so useful that they are currently the main area for research in artificial intelligence. So we will dive a little deeper into how they are built.

40 Google is a trademark of Google Inc.

CHAPTER 10

Deep Learning

The inspiration for neural networks was the neurons in the brain but artificial intelligence research has moved past a strict emulation. A real brain cell either fires or doesn't, whereas the output of a perceptron is a number. The range that number can span is governed by the activation function. Many different activation functions are used depending on the needs of the network. The only requirement is that they are not linear – the output is not simply the input amplified. That is what allows the network to make decisions; it is a vital property. The simplest activation function is called Rectified Linear Unit (ReLU) If its input is positive then it outputs the same number but if its input is negative, it outputs zero.

A neural network needs one more function. The loss function defines how wrong the network's output is while it is being trained. The network is fed an input. Then each of the weights in the network are adjusted a tiny amount in the direction that will reduce the loss.

Notice that a neural network is expected to produce its output immediately. Most of them are given a single input and produce a single output. That is very different from a brain which processes multiple continuous inputs and produces similarly continuous outputs. With a single input and output, the loss function is simple to define. The training data lists inputs and expected outputs. The network is given the input and then its output is compared to the expected output.

Going downhill

In a real brain, connections between neurons are being created and removed all the time as we learn. Each neuron has an average of seven thousand connections. In a neural network the connections are fixed; a perceptron takes inputs from every perceptron in the layer before it and sends its output to all the perceptrons in the layer after it. Those inputs are added up and the total is put through the activation function. Obviously that doesn't allow the network to learn anything. Therefore each of the inputs are multiplied by a weight. The values of all of those weights are what changes during training. A common method of training a network is called *gradient descent*.

Imagine you are on a mountain in a heavy fog. You can't see anything but you can feel the ground under your feet. You could move left or right, and forward or back. If you take little steps, you can be fairly sure that, if you follow the slope of the ground, you will end up lower down than where you started. That way you can shuffle slowly down the whole mountain.

Just as we shuffled slowly down the mountain, so many neural networks are trained the same way, reducing their loss as we reduced our altitude. Whereas our mountain has two dimensions to worry about, forward/back and left/right, a perceptron has maybe a thousand dimensions, one for each of the weights that it is training. We keep giving the network its training data, calculating a new loss and the gradients for all the weights, change the weights a tiny amount and then feed it the training data again. Over and over again. The huge number of fairly complex calculations involved in finding the gradients is why training such networks requires a massive amount of computer power.

Sequences of inputs

The connections in a neural network can only go in one direction: layer to layer from the input to the output. The method used for training the network doesn't work if connections go in the opposite direction because the mathematics becomes insoluble. However it means that the networks don't have a memory. If we are trying to analyze text or music, that is a problem; it means that every note or word has to be considered by itself. Obviously, that won't work. One thing we can do is to give a perceptron its own last output as one of its inputs. We are allowed to do that. However that doesn't give us much memory. It's more than just the previous step but the memory fades out quite quickly; it might not remember much about what happened ten notes ago. We see a similar effect with the popular Autotext game where you put the beginning of a sentence into your phone and keep accepting the words it offers you. Each word goes with the ones immediately before it but the sentence tends to lose its way.

Transformers

Another method is to completely redesign the perceptron itself. This is what a transformer network does. When a network has to deal with text, the input has to be converted to numbers. Generally each word is converted to a number. So 'aardvark' might be converted to 1, 'aardwolf' to 2 and so on. Each word goes into its own transformer but its position in the text is also put in and all the words around it. The weights of all of those inputs are then changed during training. The network learns how much weight to give to each factor in order to adequately represent a word in a valid sentence. The transformer has created an efficient coding mechanism for context.

We need to be able to calculate the loss if we are going to train such a network but how do we know what an efficient coding of a sentence looks like? Probably the majority of neural networks are trained by having two networks back to back, one encoding the input into an efficient form and the other decoding that to recreate the input data. The loss function is then simply how much the recreation differs from the original. The encoding has to be efficient because we only give it a small space and it has to contain all the features of the input data because otherwise the decoder network couldn't work.

The GPT in 'ChatGPT' stands for Generative Pre-trained Transformer. So it's something that generates, it's been trained, and it uses transformers. OpenAI isn't saying exactly how it works but it is something like this: they pre-train some transformers on a vast amount of text in order to find an efficient coding. These transformers are then used as part of a neural network that is trained against a large number of questions and answers. Given the question, it is trained to produce the corresponding answer.

Pictures

We need a different solution for images. It isn't the sequence of pixels that is important. Rather it is the relationship each pixel has with the pixels around it. To do that we can use a Convolutional Neural Network (CNN).

If you have a photo-editing application that can do blurring, sharpening and other such effects, it will be using a convolutional filter to do what you want. A pixel is just a number (or three in the case of colour pictures.) It looks at each pixel in turn, multiplies each pixel around it, including itself, by a different number and adds them all up. The result is then the value of that pixel in the resulting image. Depending on the numbers you multiply each pixel by, you get different effects. For instance you can blur or sharpen a picture by choosing different numbers.

In a CNN, we can apply multiple filters and we also often shrink the image. So an input image that is 256 pixels square might result in an output from the first layer that is 128 pixels square. From the second layer the output might be 64 pixels square, and so on. This means that the network as a whole can represent features wherever they occur in the image. Eventually the image can be shrunk down to a handful of numbers that describe the image. Maybe one of them is the probability that there is a face in the picture.

Once we have a way of detecting that there is a face in the picture, we often need to know where it is. There might be many faces and we need to know where they all are. We can split the image in two and test both of them. Given that faces are detected, we can split them again and again. Eventually we will end up with a set of rectangles, each of which exactly contain one face. Then we can tell our camera hardware to prioritize those areas when focusing and de-bluring. We can draw rectangles around them when we show the picture in the viewfinder. Or we can take each of those faces and run them through another neural network that is trained to detect people in our database of criminals.

Learning together

A Generative Adversarial Network (GAN) allows us to create two useful neural networks at the same time. One of them creates entirely new things (maybe images) that are indistinguishable from real things (maybe pictures of cats). The other network distinguishes between images that contain those things (they are pictures of cats) and images that are not.

Both networks start out completely incompetent. We feed the discriminator network some real pictures and some that are created by the generator network. The discriminator has a low loss if it can correctly decide between the two. The generator, however, has a low loss if the discriminator fails to decide correctly. Over time, the generator becomes capable of creating realistic images of things and the discriminator trains itself to recognise those things. Fun examples of what a GAN is capable of can be seen at https://thispersondoesnotexist.com, which generates photo-realistic images of people.

Deep fakes

One of the most impressive applications for neural networks has been the creation of deep fakes where videos are created of people doing and saying things that they never did or said. This is deeply questionable from an ethical standpoint but it is worth discussing how it is achieved.

You need two videos: one of the person you want to do whatever it is and another of a different person doing them. First, the videos are split into individual frames. This creates a thousand or so pictures. You run several neural networks over those images to detect faces, identify the facial features, align the faces consistently and create a mask-area where the face lies in the picture. You train CNNs on both sets to create an efficient encoding. Then the trick is to use the encoding of one set of pictures to generate images with the other set's decoder. You've got the original actor making the same facial expressions as the other actor. Now all you have to do is to superimpose it on the original video using the mask and alignment that you've already extracted. You can go through a similar process to make the second actor's words sound like the original actor said them, and then put the video and sound together.

On the job training

All of the neural networks we have seen so far are trained once and then never learn again. The network in our camera never gets any better at recognising faces than it was when it left the factory. It is often difficult or impossible to create authoritative training data. For instance the neural network might be steering a car. We need it to learn how to react in a variety of situations but we don't know what those situations are. It needs to steer smoothly around corners, which will require dozens of individual choices. Gathering sufficient data to train the network would be time-consuming and runs the risk of being incomplete.

In Reinforcement Learning, the network is given a reward when it succeeds and a punishment when it fails. For instance, when the car crashes, then the decisions it made in the last few seconds are deemed to be bad, and the ones before that, when the car was driving safely, are deemed to be good. A record is kept of every decision that the neural network made. Those decisions are played back and the weights adjusted according to whether the decision was good or bad.

Often it isn't possible to train such an application in the real world; car crashes tend to be expensive. Such applications are generally first trained on simulations but finish their training in the real world, once they can be trusted not to drive into trees at high speed.

Ethics

Neural networks require a lot of high-quality training data, hundreds of thousands of data samples, sometimes tens of millions. It is impossible for developers to collect and verify such a huge corpus. If one needed a dataset of ten million faces, it might be a good idea to take ten pictures of each model from different angles and with varying lighting, but that still means there need to be a million models and photography sessions. It would cost several million dollars, require an army of photographers and take many years.

Rather than creating such a dataset from scratch, developers scrape publicly available data from the Internet, which has probably billions of images of faces. There is a problem with that though. The data is publicly available but it is not necessarily freely licensed. Not everyone may be happy to see their vacation pictures used in an artificial intelligence dataset. If that dataset is used to train a generator, then significant parts of the training data can be seen in the generated images. For instance the artist's signature has been incorporated in generated images. If a human artist was to do that, it would be considered forgery. These are issues that must be settled in copyright law, which takes time and money to do.

The majority of the publicly available images on the Internet are of white women. There are significantly fewer images of men, let alone other skin tones. If this bias isn't addressed when selecting the training data then the resulting neural network will have a built-in bias. While software cannot be said to be racist, the effect will be the same; it will work better for white people.

The technology of deep fakes is also ethically questionable. There have been instances of celebrities' faces being superimposed on porn videos. Circulating a video of a politician making a speech that never existed could easily disrupt the democratic process. And how can actors earn a living if a movie studio can simply superimpose their face and voice on a cheaper actor?

Artificial intelligence has many open questions. Most of them are in the future but, for neural networks in particular, they are here now and we will have to find answers.

But there is no room in this book for more than a hint of the questions, let alone discussion of the answers. So we will leave neural networks now and move on to other things. A neural network is one way that a computer can be used to solve a problem that we can't. Let's look at other methods of achieving the same goal.

CHAPTER 11

Evolutionary Computing

Neural nets take their inspiration from nature, mimicking the cells that make up living brains. Genetic algorithms and evolutionary computing use the methods of natural selection to create a program that solves the problems we set it. In nature a population of organisms will usually consist of several thousand individuals at any one time. Multiple generations are generally alive at the same time. The form of each individual is stored in its chromosomes. Each chromosome contains many genes. The individuals that are the best adapted to the living conditions are more likely to reproduce. Pairs of organisms mate and their genes are mixed to create the next generation. Sometimes there are spontaneous random mutations.

Genetic algorithms do precisely the same in software. A small computer object called a chromosome is designed to represent all of the variable parameters needed to solve the problem. Each of these parameters is called a gene.

As an example we will return to the robotic insect that hid in the dark but needed to eat. We might give it two genes, one that determined how scared of light it was and the other that made it braver when it was hungry. There will often be many more genes in the chromosome. Unlike in nature, a single chromosome is used to characterize an individual; there is no advantage to be gained in using more. Initially we need a population of different individuals. A thousand or more chromosomes are created with random contents. Then they are tested to find how good they are at solving the problem. Maybe we run our robotic insects through simulated lifetimes and measure their lifespans. The most successful ones are mated in pairs and maybe some of them are mutated. The new children take the place of some of the previous generation and the process is repeated.

This may seem to be a somewhat haphazard method of reaching a solution to a problem. One does not expect random numbers to be involved in an efficient process. It might feel as if we are saying, 'Pick a number ... No not that one; try again', but in fact it settles quickly on a chromosome quite close to the solution. Of course, it might quickly settle on an answer that is only good when compared to other answers close to it. Elsewhere there might be an even better solution but no chromosomes happened to get near enough to find it. That is why mutations are used; they create genes that do not exist in the population. Most of those will be disastrous failures but occasionally they will prove to be better than anything else in the population.

The difficulty with genetic algorithms, and with evolutionary programming in general, is knowing when it has finished. Since we do not know how to solve the problem in the first place, we may not even know if an answer that we are given is as close as it is possible to get. Given time it will get as close to the answer as the genes will permit but that might take a long time and be needlessly precise. An answer to five decimal places is rarely more useful in the real world than one that is correct to four places. One can continue until

DNA carries our genetic information and composes the blueprint for life. Evolutionary computing is an attempt to reproduce the genetic behaviour, or successful mutations (known as natural selection), that occurs naturally in our DNA.

the error is below a certain amount but there is no guarantee it will ever get there; alternatively, one can run for a fixed number of generations and run the risk that the error is still too big or that it became small enough long before the run was finished. Another option would be to continue until the error is changing slowly, meaning that the algorithm is settling on an answer. However, it might only be a local solution and a mutation will soon cause it to change quickly again.

Evolution strategies

Genetic algorithms have to be implemented in a computer; they depend on having a large population of individuals in order to mate the best ones. Using a computer means that the test for competence has to be done by the computer. That might not always be possible. For example, simulating the world of our robotic insect would be difficult; we probably do not know how dangerous bright light really is. A related method called evolution strategies was devised for use when a computer-based solution is impractical.

Like genetic algorithms, a random chromosome is created containing genes, but in this case only one individual is created. The chromosome is randomly mutated. Now we have two individuals: the parent and the child. The competence of both of them is tested. If the child proves better than the parent then it is used as the basis for the next generation, otherwise the parent is used again. Evolution strategies were first invented to minimize air resistance of bodies in a wind tunnel[41] long before such things could be simulated in computer models. With the advent of sufficiently powerful computers, the evolution strategies methodology has been extended to allow multiple parents and multiple children rather like genetic algorithms.

There are two marked differences between the two approaches. In genetic algorithms (GA), the fitness of the parents determines which is permitted to breed and the children are all added to the population. In evolution strategies (ES) all parents breed but the new population is formed of the evolutionarily fittest children.

In GA the mutation rate is fixed and small. It is only used to prevent the algorithm stalling on a local maximum. In ES the mutation rate is variable and large. Although multiple parents are used to mix up the genes, mutation is seen as the main source of variability in the population. All the genes are mutated in every child. The degree to which the genes are mutated is also part of the definition of each individual and is also subject to the same process as the genes.

This produces a population of individuals that mutate faster when they are a long way from optimum, when a big change can make a big improvement, and more slowly as they approach the optimum design, when a large change is likely to produce an individual that is worse than its parents.

41 I. Rechenberg, 'Cybernetic solution path of an experimental problem', *Royal Aircraft Establishment, Library Translation* 1122, Farnborough, Hants, UK (1965).

Genetic programming

Neither genetic algorithms nor evolution strategies produce a new computer program. They merely tune the parameters of an existing program within a limited range. If the program cannot ever solve the task at hand, both approaches will fail. Genetic programming aims to overcome this limitation by allowing the whole program to be designed by natural selection.

In order to do this, we represent the program as an expression. An expression can be one of three things: a variable, such as x or y; a constant, such as 2 or π; or a function. A function looks like this:

name(expression, expression, ...)

The name of the function might be 'add' or 'multiply', for example. The number of expressions depends on what the function needs. The sine function would only require one, whereas the add function would need two. The expressions could in their turn be constants, variables or functions and so the whole thing can quickly get complicated. Pythagoras's theorem looks like this:

hypotenuse = square-root(add(square(a), square(b)))

Such a mess of parentheses makes it difficult for a human to read but computers have no such problem. It is a proven mathematical fact that any computer program can be made from such an expression, so there is no limit to the programs we can create this way. However, if we take any valid sub-expression and replace it with any other valid sub-expression, the expression as a whole is guaranteed to be valid. It will do something else of course but it will still make sense. For example, we could replace 'square(b)' in the Pythagoras's Theorem with 'add(cube(b), multiply(a, b))' and we would still have an expression that did something:

$$something\text{-}else = square\text{-}root(add(square(a),$$
$$add(cube(b), multiply(a, b))))$$

This is how genetic programming can mix two parent programs to make a child program, or in fact two child programs. It simply chooses a random expression in each parent and swaps the two expressions. Normally there are two other alternative operations that may be used. A program may be copied unchanged into the next generation or a mutation could be introduced. It is usual practice to only do one of these three alternatives to produce each individual for the next generation. This is different from genetic algorithms, where a single individual may have both mutation and crossover performed on it, and also from evolution strategies, where every chromosome is mutated.

Genetic programming is at least as useful as genetic algorithms and evolution strategies, since the programs created by them are a subset of the programs that genetic programming can design. Programs written using only simple arithmetic operations will execute quickly in a time that is directly related to the number of functions in the expression. However, in general, computer programs must contain functions that take an indeterminate time to execute, which means that we cannot even tell how long they take without actually executing them.[42] If we have a population of 1,000 individual programs and they are all taking an hour to execute, it is going to be a long, long time before we find the program that we are looking for. Of course we could impose an arbitrary limit and stop them after a short time but then there is no way to tell whether we have made our task impossible. Evolution takes time, both in the real world and in the computer. That is why biologists like the fruit fly; its short lifecycle reduces the experiment's duration. Even if 500 generations of a genetic programming project takes a long time, it is probably still short compared to the same number of fruit-fly generations. Unfortunately, programmers are not as patient as biologists.

The three techniques we have discussed – genetic algorithms, evolution strategies and genetic programming – all try to emulate natural selection and the survival of the fittest to produce a program that does what is needed without the programmer knowing in advance exactly how it is to be achieved.

---

42 Alan Turing, 'On Computable Numbers, with an Application to the *Entscheidungsproblem*', *Proceedings of the London Mathematical Society*, Series 2, vol. 42 (1937) and 43 (1938). This is Turing's most famous paper, in which he defines the Turing machine and uses it to prove the fact presented above. The paper is available online but it is highly technical and abstruse. For an explanation for the layman I recommend Charles Petzold, *The Annotated Turing* (Wiley Publishing, Inc, 2008). ISBN 978-0-470-22905-7.

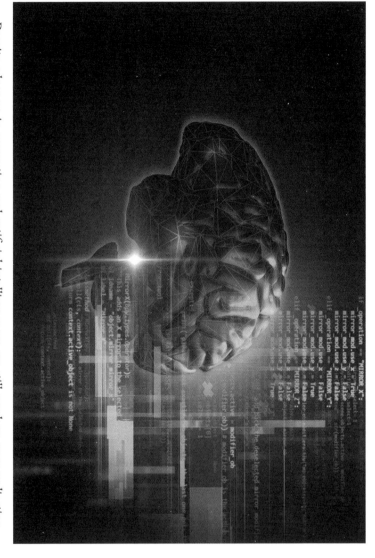

Despite advances in computing and artificial intelligence we are still nowhere near replicating the profound capacity of the human brain, much of which we still do not fully comprehend.

They have an advantage over neural networks in that once the program has been created, it should be possible to understand how it works. If we know how it works, we can be sure that it is answering the right question. Of course, as the complexity of the program increases we will be less and less able to understand it. The human body has tens of thousands of genes and nobody is able to understand it fully, even though we probably know everything we need to about basic chemistry in order to do so. The relationships between the many different chemicals involved is too complex. Similarly programs that have been created by evolutionary computing or some other automated process may become so large and entangled that they are impossible to comprehend.

Emerson Pugh[43] said, 'If the brain were so simple that we could understand it, we would be so simple we couldn't.' Should this prove to be the case, it need not prevent us from developing computer programs that are equally complex and equally difficult to understand. Even so, although such complexity wouldn't end our ambitions to create artificial intelligence, it would not be an ideal situation. One does not climb Everest in a single step; maybe we can create intelligence in many small steps that are individually trivial but combine together into something that rivals the human brain.

43 This is a difficult quote to pin down. In *Biological Origin of Human Values* (Routledge & Kegan Paul PLC, 1978), George E. Pugh attributed it to his father, Emerson, circa 1938. This is probably the earliest possible date and therefore the most likely correct attribution.

CHAPTER 12

Intelligent Agents

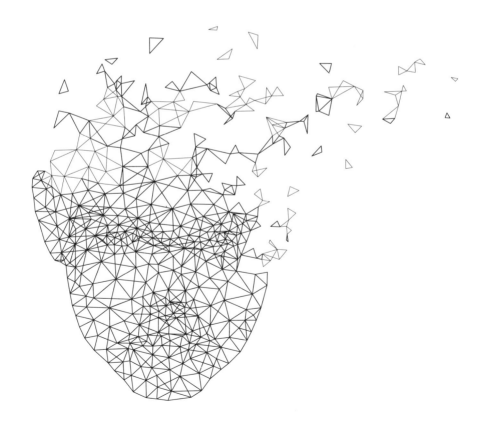

So far most of the artificial intelligence systems that we have discussed have been single large programs. While initial experimental implementations have proven successful, many of them have proven impossible to scale up to a useful size because they become too big and too slow. Other approaches offer the capability to grow larger at the expense of being difficult or impossible to understand. Intelligent agents were developed to address both of these issues. They allow complexity to emerge from the interactions between many simple programs. Since the programs themselves are small and their range of actions is limited, the whole system should be comprehensible.

In the social sciences, an intelligent agent is a person or other system that is rational and autonomous and which acts on information it perceives about the world to carry out actions that affect the world. The same definition holds with the agents we will be exploring here. The agent must be rational; it must make good decisions based on the information it has available. It is autonomous; its decisions are the result of its perceptions of the world and its own experience. Its relationship to the world includes some process of perceiving it. It is not expected to have perfect and complete information in the same way a chess program does, so part of its task will be understanding its environment. It must then act. Its actions will change the environment, which will change its perceptions, and it must continue to operate in this changed world.

Co-operation within a system

So far this might more or less describe most of the programs that we have discussed up until now, although most of them tend to exist inside simulated worlds because perception is rather hard to do. However, intelligent agents have one more defining characteristic; they are not alone. In the social sciences, intelligent agents are used in models of how society works together.

A company that makes mobile phones is composed of several different departments. The research and development (R&D) division designs a new phone, the production department makes it and the sales team sells it. The marketing people advertise it and the executives make sure they are all doing the right things. All these departments need to talk to each other if the company is going to be successful. R&D needs input from marketing and sales if they are to design something people will want to buy, and from production to make sure that what they design can be built. Sales needs to know from production how much a product costs to produce if they are to sell it at a profit, and from marketing how much the public will be able to afford. There will be many different designs in progress at any time and production will be making several different models. They need to be told by the executives which designs to prioritize and how many of each model to make.

In AI multiple intelligent agents work together in a single system. Like the mobile phone company they each have a particular job to do that they are uniquely capable of doing.

To carry out that task, they need to talk with the other agents that are doing different jobs. Each agent perceives its environment but that does not mean that they can see the AI lab outside the computer. Their environment is defined by their task. For an agent tasked with walking on a thick carpet, its environment is position and force signals coming from its legs. It does not need to know, or care, whether it is moving towards food or away from light; it is concerned only with moving its legs so as to move efficiently in whichever direction it has been told that it needs to move.

An intelligent agent system is similar to subsumption architecture in that it is composed of multiple self-contained modules. However, the strict rules under which the subsumption architecture operates are substantially relaxed. Intelligent agents are allowed to have memory, they are not limited to communicating only by repressing other agents and they do not have to take input solely from the real world. As a result, they may be more complex than the simple reflex actions that a subsumption architecture behaviour implements. Both an agent and a behaviour do one thing but the thing that an agent does can be significantly smarter.

Consider our robot insect hiding in the dark. So far we have been considering its higher brain functions but in the real world, with a real robot, there are other considerations. Does it have legs or wheels? How does it perceive its environment? Having perceived it, how does it come to the realization that there is food out there but also bright light? Having decided to move towards the food, how does it navigate from here to there? Does it need to walk differently depending on the floor surface? How does it recognize and avoid obstacles?

All these questions have been asked by artificial intelligence researchers at one time or another and all of them have been solved at least to some extent. However, they are all very different problems with different solutions.

Navigation might be best solved by making a map of the insect's surroundings, maybe by making use of frames. Walking on various surfaces might be a good use of genetic algorithms, while recognizing food and light could be best implemented with a neural network. Above all of these will be the superego of the insect, deciding whether to move towards the food or away from the light and that might be implemented in fuzzy logic. By making each of these tasks into a self-contained intelligent agent, we can implement each one using whatever method seems best suited to its needs.

Intelligent agents can be categorized depending on how they operate. Reflex agents have no memory; they simply choose an action to take depending on what their senses are saying at the present time. The agent in charge of our insect's sight might be like this: it detects objects purely by what they look like from instant to instant. A more advanced organism might be able to build up a map of the world from different viewpoints but that is not necessary for our robot beetle. Model-based reflex agents have a memory. They build a model of the world outside to which their senses can add. The actions they take are chosen based on their model of the world. The insect's legs might work like this: the robot needs to know what it is doing in order to make its next action and it might learn that the surface it is walking on is soft or irregular and make adjustments to how it operates based on that information. Goal-based agents are searching for a way to achieve some task that is not immediately attainable. They have to plan a sequence of actions that will result in them being successful. The mapping agent in our robot might work like that. It needs to plan a route to food or darkness that avoids obstacles and, rather than heading directly towards its ultimate goal, it might first need to move away from it in order to reach it.

The final category is utility-based agents. These operate not with a fixed goal but with the objective of achieving the most 'utility'. If one were to anthropomorphize more than computer scientists are comfortable doing, we might say that they want to make themselves as happy as possible. The superego of our robot might work like this. It wants to keep the robot well fed and safe. It will need to trade off one of these from time to time to ensure the other.

All of these independent programs need to talk to each other and this is generally done by passing messages. The intelligent agent responsible for the senses will tell the mapping agent that there is light or food. The superego will tell the mapping agent that it wants to move towards the nearest food. Then the mapping agent calculates the best route and tells the walking agent which direction to move. A message is a block of data that is sent either to one particular agent or to all of them. The block contains just that information that is necessary. If the robot's sight agent needs to tell the mapping agent that there is food 30 centimetres (1 foot) to the north, it only needs three pieces of data: food, 30 centimetres (1 foot), north. If a message is sent to more than one agent, only the agents that are equipped to make use of a message will process it, the others will ignore it; the walking agent neither cares where food may be found nor has the capability to do anything with the information.

Stock market analysts

Another use for intelligent agent systems is in the stock market. Agents are used to analyze the market and generate buy and sell order recommendations, or even to buy and sell directly. There might be individual agents to monitor the market and generate statistics, to detect anomalous price movements, to find shares that are good to buy or sell, to manage the overall risk represented by the user's portfolio and to interact with the user.

There is one more feature that we can add to our agents: the ability to learn. Because they are situated in the real world and receive feedback on the results of their actions, we can have them adjust their behaviour according to how successful their past decisions have been. The agent responsible for walking can learn to navigate carpet or wooden floors, and the agent responsible for predicting future stock movements can modify its calculations according to whether the stock price actually rises or falls.

Stock market analysts scrutinizing the fluctuations of data. In the future, this could potentially be a job exclusively performed by artificial intelligence.

This is still one program; we have made it a program of independent modules – they might even be running on different computers – but they work with each other in a hierarchy that we have designed. However, by making each part discrete, the complexity of each is reduced. Just as it is difficult to pat your head and rub your stomach at the same time, a computer program is harder to write and maintain if it has to do more than one thing simultaneously. While the whole program is still complex, that complexity is compartmentalized. We can modify a module without affecting any others.

CHAPTER 13

Swarm Intelligence

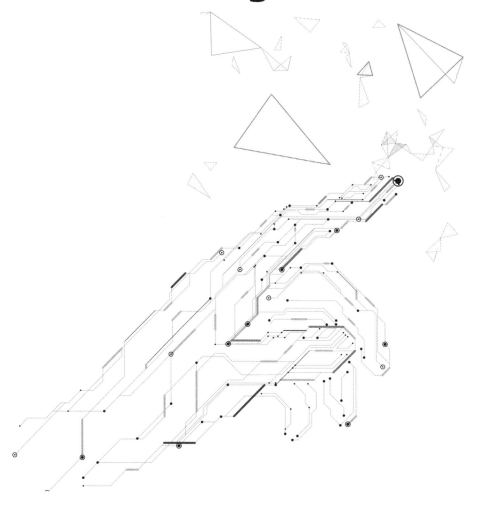

Ants live in a highly efficient and well-ordered society. Everything they do, they do in pretty much the most efficient manner: their nests are constructed to maintain the optimum temperature and ventilation; when they find a food source the path they take to it is the fastest available. One might see this and assume that some central authority, maybe the queen, was controlling all of the activity. In fact there is no such authority. The queen is nothing but an egg-laying machine. Every ant is an autonomous individual, acting at all times according to a few simple rules.

Ant trails

When an ant is looking for food, it will wander about randomly unless it finds the pheromone trail left by another ant returning to the nest with food. Then it tends to follow the trail. The stronger the trail is, the more likely it is to follow it. When it finds food it will return to the nest, laying down its own trail. If there is a lot of food available in that location, many ants will return the same way and the trail will get stronger and more attractive to any ant that stumbles across it. Nevertheless, some ants will lose the trail from time to time and take a different path. If that path is shorter, then more ants can travel along it at the same time and it will get more pheromones, while the pheromones on the older trail will evaporate. Over time, the path that the individuals take comes closer and closer to the optimum.

Using such examples from nature as templates for similar behaviours in artificial intelligence is called swarm intelligence. We can use swarm intelligence to design a group of robots. The robots will be simple in themselves with knowledge about the environment local to them and, often, communicate only with those others that are close by. Each device is autonomous; there is no central intelligence telling it what to do. Like the robots we discussed when talking about the subsumption architecture, each individual only knows what it senses about the world. This allows us to create robust behaviours that adapt automatically to changes in the environment. When we have a large number of identical robots with the same programming, we achieve even more resilience, since the failure of any small number of individuals will make little difference to the efficiency of the whole.

Such robots, with behaviour very similar to that of an ant, could be used to find and remove landmines or search disaster areas for casualties. Ants use pheromones to signal to other members of the nest, but sensing such things is not easy for robots (although it has been done). Lights, sounds or short-range radio are used in their place.

Search robots

Imagine a large number of robots in a hiking area. In the absence of anything else to do, they position themselves so that they are in the centre of all the other robots they can see, with the

Ants solve complex problems using simple behaviours.

result that they are distributed evenly over the landscape. They might be attracted to loud noises or a waving gesture, so hikers who found themselves in difficulty could ask for help.

If required, a request for emergency services can be passed from robot to robot until it reaches one that can get a signal through via radio or mobile phone. If it is necessary to transport the hiker, more robots can be called to help and the others will move positions to maintain coverage. All of that could be implemented with little more than the subsumption architecture.

Birds flocking

The other frequently emulated swarm behaviour is flocking, like birds. It is used when the whole flock needs to move together but also to search for some objective. The rules for creating a flock of individuals are very simple:

- Stay close to other members of the flock.
- Fly in the direction that is the average of directions being flown by those members that are nearby.
- Maintain a safe distance from other members and other obstacles.

If we add to those the tendency to turn towards some objective, the entire flock will be drawn towards it.

Search 'copters

If we return to our hiking area example, this time we might decide to protect our hikers with a flock of quadcopters. These

A flock of starlings search for the best roost.

aircraft patrol the area in a flock but are attracted by the colour bright orange, which hikers often wear. Maybe there is someone hurt where they are difficult to see. A few of the quadcopters might notice a flash of orange and turn towards it. As the flock flies over the hiker each of them will be watching from a slightly different vantage point so more and more will see the casualty. Soon the entire flock will be circling low in that one spot – the swarm has successfully located an object of interest. Other artificial intelligence technologies would be needed, such as natural language understanding, gesture recognition and image recognition but, as we have seen, those are not intractable problems.

Bee swarming

When a bee colony has been so successful that it has outgrown its present hive, the queen and more than half the workers leave it to look for a new home. The swarm finds a temporary location in a tree while scouts go out to look for prospective new nest sites. When they return, they tell the swarm about the place they have found by performing a waggle dance. At first there will be many prospective sites being suggested but over time the better sites are supported by more scouts until finally a consensus is reached and the whole swarm goes to the site of the new hive and moves in.

Let's copy that technique for finding a good hotel in Manhattan for a large group of tourists. Many of the group are old or infirm and cannot walk far. We can set up a temporary

A swarm of bees congregates in a tree while its scouts look for a new home.

base at the bandstand in Central Park and send out our fittest members to scout. They return to the bandstand and compare notes. When the scouts hear about a hotel that seems to be better than the one they found they go and take a look at it. Eventually a consensus is formed and everyone goes to the chosen hotel and books in.

Manhattan has a regular street plan with roads called 'streets' at right angles to roads called 'avenues', so when, scouts return they only have to say which street and which avenue the hotel is closest to for everyone to know where it is. We can represent the location of a scout at any time by two numbers: street and avenue or, in mathematics language, X and Y. If we wanted to, we could have a piece of graph paper at the bandstand and track the progress of each scout and the hotels found on it. The scouts' search for a hotel on the streets and avenues of Manhattan is the same as a search for some optimal value on an X, Y graph.

Swarming without robots

When we were discussing genetic algorithms, each individual in the population was represented by a set of numbers we called genes. The genetic algorithm was a way of changing these numbers until they represented the optimal individual.

Using the techniques of swarm intelligence, we can take those same numbers but, instead of seeing them as genes in a chromosome, we can think of them as positions in space, on a graph or on a map. As an individual moves around in space, the numbers change, just as when you are walking around in

Manhattan the numbers of the street and the avenue you are on change. Rather than a process of evolution between fixed individuals, our search is now represented by the journey of individuals. We can implement that search using any of the techniques that we have found for searching space – such as ants foraging, bees swarming or birds flocking – without having to build any robots at all.

Product launch

An example might make that clearer. A supermarket chain wants to introduce a new product but they don't know how to price it or how much shelf space to give it. The price and the size of the display would be the two numbers that defined the search space. A position in the space is defined by a price and a size, just as on a graph a position is defined by an X co-ordinate and a Y co-ordinate. Each supermarket in the chain picks a position – a price and a size – in that space at random and varies them from day to day, maybe following the bird-flocking rules but tending to be attracted to a larger profit. The flock tends to stick together but it is spread out over the space so it can see all the profits available all around it. Or maybe they use the ant model, so when supermarkets make a good profit one day they drop a metaphorical scent marker. Supermarkets that get close to the same values tend to move towards them. When multiple supermarkets have had good experiences with certain values the scent will be stronger and attract others from further away. Or maybe they act like swarming bees; each supermarket searches by itself for the best profit and reports the best it has found. Then it picks something promising from the reports of the other supermarkets and tries that. When there is agreement where the best profits are to be found, everyone uses that price and size.

It does not only work with two values such as price and size, of course. The same method will work with three, four or dozens of numbers. The individuals will be wandering around a multidimensional space, which is difficult to imagine but the mathematics is straightforward. We don't actually have to create that space, just vary some numbers and measure the distances between points. We measure distance using Pythagoras's Theorem and it works in any number of dimensions.[44]

If we have a problem for which a computer can test solutions, we can implement the entire process inside the computer. Perhaps we have a new algorithm for compressing files but it is dependent on several numbers and we don't know what values to choose to get the best compression ratio. We can use those numbers as the co-ordinates of a space and simulate many individuals searching through that space for

---

44 Maths is often beautiful, and this is one of the most satisfying results. The distance between two points on a two-dimensional graph is easily shown to be the square root of (difference in X)^2 + (difference in Y)^2 simply by drawing the triangle on the graph. If we have a three-dimensional graph, it can be shown almost as easily that the distance between two points is the square root of (difference in X)^2 + (difference in Y)^2 + (difference in Z)^2. We can keep adding dimensions as much as we like.

the best compression ratios. Like the supermarkets searching for price and size in the real world, we can use any swarm intelligence methods we like.

CHAPTER 14

Data-mining and Statistics

There is a lot of data available these days. When CDs were first invented, a single one could hold all the text of the *Encyclopaedia Britannica* (although not the pictures). Even with 44 million words spread over 30 large volumes, it was less than 400 megabytes. A modern PC has a hard disk 2,500 times bigger than that – 1 terabyte, enough to store 2 million books. It has been estimated that there is around 10 billion times that amount of data stored in the world's computers today and it doubles every year. Much of it would be of great use for various purposes if some way could be found to extract those parts of interest.

On a smaller scale, a large retail chain may have data on the buying habits of millions of their customers. Social media and other Internet service providers have data on millions of their subscribers. But data, the raw figures on who bought what and when, is next to useless.

Data is not information and information is not knowledge. Making sense of the data (turning it into information) and making use of it (turning into knowledge) is a monumental task. If a human was to process the data from 1 million individuals, and took only ten seconds on each, he or she would still take a year to finish. Since one individual might buy a few dozen products a week, the results would be a year out of date by the time they were produced. Of course, computers are used for tasks that take humans too long but in this case we don't always know what we want the computer to look for.

Data is stored in applications called databases, which have built-in capabilities to analyze the data and present it in different forms as required by its users. We can find how many of our customers bought milk. If they have loyalty cards we can even find out how many women under the age of 40 bought milk.[45] Given sufficient time and enough intuition we can find useful patterns in the data that will let us make profitable changes to how we do business. However, there is only so much time and intuition that can be spent productively; generating these sorts of associations automatically is far more attractive.

Decision trees

All artificial intelligence methods are applied to data-mining, especially neural networks and fuzzy logic, but there are a few that are particular to it. One such technique is decision trees. The computer finds the single datum that best predicts

---

45 Before the invention of loyalty cards, one had to track individual customers by their bankcard numbers. But the same customer might use a debit card most of the time but switch to a credit card towards the end of the month and pay cash for small purchases. This is, of course, the real reason for the existence of loyalty cards. The ones that are common to multiple companies provide even more information on their subjects' habits; supermarkets can find out how many times their customers visit the cinema and so forth. If you are getting something for nothing, the chances are good that someone is making money from your data.

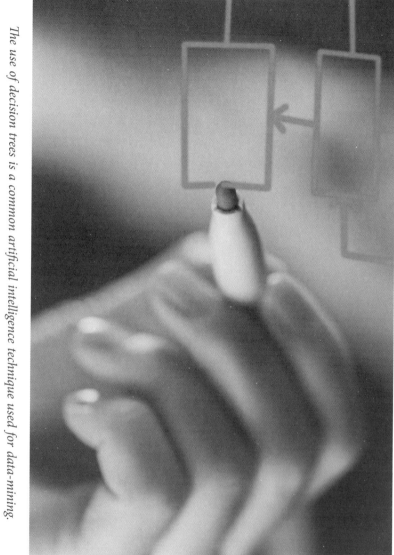

The use of decision trees is a common artificial intelligence technique used for data-mining. It can be useful in market targeting, locating the most relevant data to predict an outcome.

the outcome. If we were interested in finding the demographic of people who buy spaghetti, we can split our database by those who buy it and those who don't, then check each of the data we have on those individuals to find the most uneven split. We might find the most discriminating datum was the gender of the purchaser[46] – men might buy more spaghetti than women do. We can split the database on gender and go through the same process with each half independently.

The computer might find that age is more discriminating among men but average income is more discriminating among women. We can continue the process and make our profiles more specific until the amount of data in each category is too small to be useful. Our marketing department would be interested to learn that 30 per cent of the spaghetti was bought by men in their 20s and 20 per cent by professional women. It would be profitable to target those demographics with advertising and special offers. They are unlikely to be as pleased to learn that 5 per cent is bought by unmarried men in their 20s with a university degree.

Market basket analysis

Another popular technique is market basket analysis. This allows us to find the products that are most often bought together. Suppose, for example, that our analysis finds that many of the customers who bought spaghetti also bought

---

46 This is purely an example. Real life almost certainly doesn't work this way.

pasta sauce. If we found that a certain individual bought spaghetti and not the sauce, we could offer them a discount on sauce on their next visit. We can also optimize the placement of products to ensure that our customers can find the goods they want but have to walk past possible impulse-buys to do so.

The problem with market basket analysis is the huge number of possible combinations of products that we need to consider. A reasonably large outlet might have tens of thousands of product lines; even to consider all possible pairs of products we would have to consider hundreds of millions of possibilities and for combinations of three the numbers go into trillions. This is obviously not going to be practical. There are two ways we can make the task tractable. One way is to define our product categories more broadly. We might bundle all purchases of frozen fish together, rather than worrying whether it was Dover sole in lemon flavour crust or chip shop battered cod that our customers bought. Similarly we might consider only bulk beer and speciality beer rather than tracking every brand individually.

The other way is to only consider the products that are bought by a sufficient number of customers. If only 10 per cent of our clientele buy nappies, any combination of nappies with other products can only be bought by at most 10 per cent. Having cut the number of products we are considering down by a significant degree we can consider all pairs of them and again forget about any that are not bought by enough people.

Now we have pairs of products we can save even more time when making combinations of three. We need only consider merging pairs that have a product in common. For example, if we know that people buy beer and wine together and also that they buy beer and snacks together, we can consider whether they buy beer, wine and snacks together. In the next step we can merge combinations of three that have two items in common, and so on. At each step we discard any combinations that an insufficient number of people purchase.

Bayesian networks

It is useful to know which data often occur together, but sometimes we need to have a better understanding of why that happens. Suppose we are running that dating agency again and we want to know what makes a successful match. We have our database of all our clients and the results of the feedback forms we give them to rate their experiences.

We might wonder if two tall people get along better than two people who have a large difference in height. We form a hypothesis that a difference in height affects the probability of a successful date. There is a statistical method for checking this type of hypothesis called Bayesian networks, the maths for which becomes truly horrendous but can be automated with relative ease.

At its core is Bayes's Theorem, which is a formula for converting a value of the probability of this data (given this hypothesis) into the value of the probability of this hypothesis (given this data).[47] To use it in this case, we make two competing hypotheses. One states that two of our pieces of data affect one another and the other states that they are independent. We calculate the probabilities of the two hypotheses given the data that we have collected and adopt the most likely as our belief.

It is worth noting that we cannot tell which piece of data is the cause and which is the effect; so far as the maths is concerned, having a successful relationship may make people the same height, although other factors may persuade us otherwise. It also doesn't prove that there is a causal link, only that the data implies there is a relationship between them. There might be another factor that links the two that we may not be considering or even recording, or the data may have occurred in that way purely by chance.

Given the power of computers, we do not have to devise every possible hypothesis manually. We can test all possible hypotheses. In this case we are unlikely to keep more than 20 characteristics on our clients and so there are only that number of hypotheses to check. If we think two characteristics might interact to affect the result, we would have another 380, which is still reasonable. With four the workload goes up by 6,840, which is probably OK since we have plenty of time but, if this was something a robot was doing to interact with the real world, we might struggle to get the calculations and database accesses done quickly enough.

47 The formula is P(H | D) = P(D | H) . P(H) / P(D) where | is read as 'given', P( ) is read as 'the probability of', H is the hypothesis and D is the data.

Market basket analysis and Bayesian networks are both machine learning techniques. While the machine is certainly uncovering information that was previously unknown, there is disagreement about whether this is real learning or merely mathematics. If we do an addition sum, can we really be said to have learned that 2+2=4, or merely applied a known technique?

There is an apocryphal tale about a man who had a bomb drop onto his house at the precise moment that he flushed the toilet. It was clear to everyone, him included, that his actions did not cause the bomb to drop. However, it still took two years before he again dared to flush a toilet. We said above that a correlation does not prove causation. Just because people of similar height have more successful encounters, we cannot assume that being of similar height causes success. However, the human brain does not seem to operate that way. Deep down it appears that we are wired to assume causality whenever we see a correspondence. If Bayesian networks do the same, we might see that as indicating that we are on the right track.

CHAPTER 15

Forwards from the Cutting Edge

Artificial intelligence affects all our lives more than any of us know: intelligent agents buy and sell shares on the stock market; neural networks detect when our credit cards have been stolen; the online assistant on our bank's website may be a chatbot; aeroplanes fly and land[48] automatically; our mobile phones talk back to us and focus their cameras automatically on human faces. All of these and many more are built using technology from the field of artificial intelligence. However, the ultimate goal is not here yet. We have no android friends with whom we can converse. We have no robot housemaids.

The attempts to create general intelligence foundered in the 1980s but retrenched and began moving down a different path. Because it is too difficult to construct an accurate and detailed model of the world, these new technologies make the world its own model. They are embedded in robots that interact with the world and learn from it. Artificial intelligence is not proceeding along a single path towards a human-like brain; all of its many technologies are being developed at the same time for use in a multitude of fields, from call centres to Martian

48 Aircraft can take off, fly and land themselves, most of the time. Almost all landings are in fact manual. Flight is more or less solved; it's the unexpected events that mean there still needs to be a human pilot, and such events occur on every flight. On the other hand, if the pilot must land in dense fog or the aircraft is a drone with a low cost of failure, the capability is there.

exploration. Simultaneously, others are working on the techniques that will be needed when artificial intelligence advances further.

Robots and prosthetic limbs

The Actroid series of robots developed by Osaka University are highly detailed replicas of humans. They are immobile because much of their machinery is external to the body. Nevertheless they are able to mimic human mannerisms and expressions, and maintain eye contact.

Robots are being built that can swim like cuttlefish, fly like birds and wriggle like snakes. The MIT Cheetah can run at high speed and jump over obstacles.

There are now prototypes of prosthetic arms[49] that are interfaced to the nerves or directly to the brain.[50] They are somewhat clumsy and there is a learning process where the neural net in the arm learns how to interpret signals from the user's brain and, one assumes, the user's brain learns how to generate the right signals.

Prosthetic limbs are also driving the creation of self-contained and agile robot hardware. A robot will not complain

---

49 Max Ortiz-Catalan et. al. 'An Osseointegrated Human-machine Gateway for Long-term Sensory Feedback and Motor Control of Artificial Limbs', *Science Translational Medicine 8* October, 2014: vol. 6, issue 257, 257re6 DOI: 10.1126/scitranslmed.3008933.

50 J. Andrew Pruszynski and Jörn Diedrichsen 'Reading the Mind to Move the Body', *Science* (22 May, 2015): 860–61.

The MIT Cheetah on an athletics field at the Massachusetts Institute of Technology. MIT scientists said the robot, modeled after the fastest land animal, may have real-world applications, including for prosthetic legs.

if we attach a poorly designed arm to it that either grips too firmly or moves too slowly but a human amputee certainly will. Humans will know immediately if the device does not allow them to make the correct actions. If we program a false leg to run, the wearer will be aware if it does not allow him to use the appropriate gait in common or even rare circumstances, whereas the problem may never occur in the laboratory and if it does it may not be apparent. Such expert testing is invaluable. Amputees, or their insurance companies, will also be willing to pay a significant amount of money for the right device and a large marketplace drives costs down.

When the idea of robots first arose, people imagined that they would take over all the menial jobs that humans had to do. It was assumed that human intellect was all but unattainable, while simply understanding the world was trivial, something that any animal could do. But it was the intellectual tasks that fell to automation first. A computer still cannot talk like a human but it can beat any person on the planet at chess. In fact it is those menial, unskilled jobs that have proved the hardest for a robot to perform. The abilities that we take for granted – recognizing objects in the world around us; understanding and responding in natural spoken language; handling the multitude of unexpected circumstances, so trivial that we do not even notice – are the ones that are most difficult to implement in a machine.

RepliéeQ1-expo, an example of a working Actroid robot at
Expo 2005 in Aichi, Japan.

Working robots

While it might be possible to create a robot hotel maid now, it would be confused by the first guest who left a towel on the shower rail to dry, broke a glass in the basin or left their suitcase open on the bed. On the other hand, semi-skilled jobs such as car construction were mostly automated decades ago using very rudimentary robots with hardly any intelligence. Even highly skilled jobs, such as those in the stock market and finance houses, are being augmented if not replaced by artificial intelligences. Where jobs are the sole preserve of humans it is generally because of those basic skills, that every five year-old human has, to understand language and the world around it. It is certain that in the years to come robots and artificial intelligence technology will take over more tasks that we believe require human intelligence. However, as new technologies are developed they create new jobs that require human intelligence; for example, no one made a living as a web designer before the World Wide Web was invented, and few had the opportunity to produce videos at home for a worldwide audience.

There are three areas where we may expect to see artificial intelligence progress in the near future. The expert systems, chatbots and intelligent devices will continue to become more prevalent and smarter. As the expert systems and the natural language parsers they use become more foolproof, we will begin to see chatbots that converse with members of the public in narrowly defined subjects, such as in call centres. So long as you don't try to ask them about the weather, they will be able to advise you every bit as well as the humans they will replace. Our mobile phones will have capabilities that seem like magic and be more connected to every aspect of our lives and the devices we use. Even now, smartphone apps can connect to our other various devices to instruct the TV to record a programme or to switch the central heating on. If we add artificial intelligence into the mix, we get TVs that suggest programmes we may want to watch, and central heating systems that learn our daily routine and calculate how to provide for our needs efficiently. Prosthetics will become almost as good as the limb or organ they replace. The Bluetooth headset has let us become used to seeing people apparently talking to themselves in public; Apple's Siri and similar apps now implement a simple information search function, although often they fall back on providing a list of websites that might hold the information we are looking for. With more powerful computers and more advanced techniques in natural language parsing and speech recognition, they will be able to understand the websites themselves, and understand us well enough to know what piece of information we need. We will soon have intelligent research assistant apps, while game and personal assistant apps will allow us to interact with our devices using only spoken language.

Video games

An often-neglected field in artificial intelligence is video games. When the first 'shooter' games were released, the monsters simply moved towards the player's position. Later they would take advantage of cover when it was available. Now they will act as a team and attempt to outflank the player. These actions are far more advanced than anything that has ever been implemented in a robot.

Games offer a perfect environment for developing the higher levels of intelligent behaviour. The attempts to address these functions in the 1980s failed because the real world is too complex to model in a computer. Even if the computer is powerful enough, the model is too large and complex ever to be typed in to it. But a game world is restricted and the characters can have a full model of how it works and what can happen in it. In a game, the size and complexity of the model is not an issue. In the future, the games that we play on our computers and phones will feature more natural interactions. The characters will have lives of their own rather than following a predefined schedule and they will think and plan for themselves. We will be able to speak to computer-controlled characters and have them answer us with realistic mannerisms and simulated emotions. There will be a limit, of course; we will not be able to talk to them about absolutely anything, only subjects that have relevance to the game, but that will seem natural; we do not expect perfection in a game.

Future AI

All of this will be achieved using the artificial intelligence technologies that we have seen but with no attempt to create a thinking machine. Like the Chinese room, they will use lots of rules to make it seem as if they are intelligent. However, strong artificial intelligence will be progressing from the insect-like robots we have now, up the evolutionary ladder until we have something as intelligent as a mammal, maybe a dog or possibly just a squirrel. They will start to find uses in disaster response and other dangerous, low-skill niches.

In around 30 years, we will have computers with the same processing power as the human brain, and maybe ten or 20 years later we will have that same processing power on our desks and then in our pockets. At about the same time, we probably will be able to construct robots that operate in the real world at least as well as a rather unintelligent human does. They will use the same sort of techniques as the human nervous system uses for its lower-level functions, although the rest may owe rather more to computer science than neurobiology. For that reason it will be obvious that they are not alive or conscious. Nevertheless, we will find ourselves talking to them as if they are people and talking about them as if they are conscious. They will find employment in repetitive tasks in familiar surroundings where there are few surprises. Even so they will get confused often and frequently be more trouble than they are worth. Such is the bane of cutting-edge technology.

Creating a true artificial intelligence requires more than a fast computer with lots of memory. It will take research into the operation of the brain, which will need more advanced scanning and probing instruments, and research into techniques, which will involve lots of trial and error building prototypes. All that will take time but nobody can say how much. My personal feeling is that 30 years is too short and that an artificial intelligence that operates the same way as our brain works won't be developed before the second half of the 21st century. But it probably will be before the century ends. Such a mind could be used for many tasks for which humans are not ideal, such as space exploration, but they will suffer from many of the same disadvantages as humans. In all probability it is the ability to create connections between disparate subjects that allows us to solve unexpected problems. A mind like ours will have stray thoughts and emotions because that is an indispensable feature of how our minds work. Artificial intelligences will daydream and enjoy a beautiful sunset. They will get bored and over-tired. They will make mistakes and need to learn skills, at which they will be as effective as a human. They will need time off to achieve a work-life balance.

We might find that strong artificial intelligence is impossible but that would not prevent robots from becoming as intelligent as humans; it only means that they would lack consciousness. Given sufficient computing power, weak artificial intelligence is enough.

Peering into the mists of the future it is impossible to be sure of anything. Some technologies arrive out of nowhere and change our lives dramatically without notice. Strong artificial intelligence is a field that we can see looming out of the fog a long way ahead of us. We can be almost certain that the road we are on will get there eventually and when we do get there it will be a revolutionary technology but we still do not know how many twists and turns the road takes, exactly how far we have to go or what it will look like when we get there. We have guesses, some of them are utopian, some are dystopian, but they are only guesses.

CHAPTER 16

Can Machines Think?

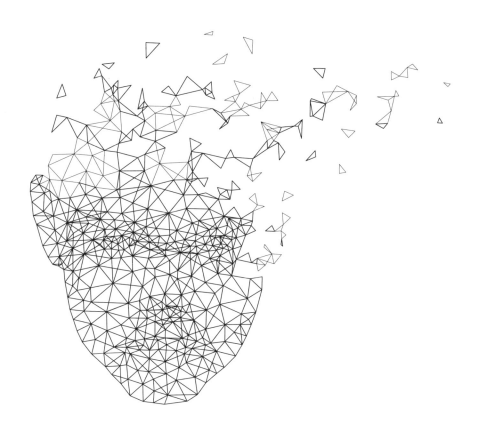

Weak AI or what I have termed Pragmatic AI is sufficient for any needs we may have. If an artificial mind is capable of everything a human can do, it doesn't matter if it is conscious or not. We can still have robot housemaids and nannies. We can send robots to the stars on journeys that last decades because we can put them to sleep and wake them up easily. We can give them dangerous jobs because there are no ethical dilemmas involved in getting them killed. Nevertheless, the prospect of a truly conscious robot is fascinating and exciting – or maybe scary and repulsive, depending on one's attitude.

In 1965 Gordon Moore, a founder of the Intel corporation, observed that the number of transistors in an integrated circuit (a 'chip' in modern informal parlance) doubled every year. In 1975, he revised his estimate to a doubling every two years. Intel executive David House suggested it might be closer to 18 months. Since the number of components in a circuit is a good indication of the power of the circuit, and therefore the computing power of a computer made from it, computers have continued to get more and more powerful over the decades since, approximately in line with what is called 'Moore's Law'. A major contribution to this advancement has been that the companies involved have based their plans on Moore's Law, making it something of a self-fulfilling prophecy.

If this exponential increase in computing power continues only another few decades, computers will soon have the same power as the human brain.

This is a sobering fact but, in itself, it is not particularly important. We have had fast computers for a long time. Even pocket calculators are capable of doing arithmetic faster than humans. A computer as powerful as the human brain still needs a program. We might be able to make high-definition animated movies at home that are indistinguishable from reality but that would not shake the foundations of our world.

If we knew exactly how the human brain works, we could simulate it in a computer and it would work precisely the same as if it were a natural brain. Maybe in a few decades we might be able to do that but right now we do not know enough about the brain to write the program. Of course, we would also have to provide sensors and actuators to simulate the rest of the body, and that is also beyond our current capability. We cannot simply connect a human brain, either real or simulated, to laser range-finders, CCD cameras, microphones, pneumatic cylinders and electric motors; the brain has evolved to process data from eyes and ears, and to control a specific set of muscles. Perhaps we shouldn't expect to be able to build a human brain in a computer but rather an entirely new intelligence with different senses and effectors. Such a mind will be entirely alien to us, more so than any existing creature.

Bertrand Russell (1872–1970) whose Principia Mathematica,
sought to codify the operation of mathematical logic.

Is it possible to make a computerized brain?

There are two objections to the likelihood of being able to reproduce the brain in a computer. The first is that the brain, while important, is not the seat of consciousness. Rather, it is the soul that makes humans what they are. Here I will defer to Turing, who pointed out that a benevolent god would surely create souls for those creatures whose brains were sufficiently powerful. Any further argument must lie in the field of theology, into which I am not going to stray. The second caveat is that we are assuming that the brain does stuff that can be simulated in a computer and maybe that is not so. While this may seem innocent on the surface, it has ramifications that threaten everything we know about the world.

In 1910–13 Alfred North Whitehead and Bertrand Russell published *Principia Mathematica*, which sought to codify the operation of mathematical logic. We do not know of any mathematics with greater power and there is no reason to believe that such a thing exists. It laid down the laws for how mathematics works and, by extension, how physics, chemistry and every other science operates. It is just one of a multitude of possible formal systems that can be constructed to do the same, so at first sight it may not appear important. However, in 1936, Alan Turing and Alonzo Church proved that all of these systems were equivalent; one might be more or less expressive than another in certain fields and therefore useful but they were all capable of expressing the same truths and they all failed in certain particular cases.[51] The operation of computers is one such formal system. A computer language is equivalent to *Principia Mathematica* and every other form of maths. It is capable of expressing the same truths as any other mathematical language and it fails in precisely the same ways. Since brains are made of physical matter and operate according to the laws of physics, if the human brain is doing something that computers cannot there must be an extension to the laws of physics and mathematics that makes it possible. This addition to science would define a formal system that is more powerful than any other that we know about. If we found such a thing it would have repercussions throughout all of science. It would change the world, all by itself.

Of course, when we found this new maths we could make our computers capable of using it. Even if we had to build nerve cells in the laboratory and make our computers out of those, technology will eventually be sufficiently advanced to make it possible. It is far more likely that we could extract the principle on which the magic depends and reimplement it in our computers.

51 It was a shock to the mathematics community back in the 1930s that there were truths that could never be proved; but they recovered from their outrage and investigated thoroughly. We now know precisely what these cases are and why they are unprovable. They are not the sort of things that human brains can solve either.

Simulation is not duplication

When John Searle proposed his Chinese room argument, he was asserting only that artificial intelligence could not be made by manipulating symbols – by a book of rules – but it has far wider application, as he himself agrees. The book of rules could just as easily be implementing a neural net or subsumption architecture, or a simulation of a human brain. Searle's argument is that simulation is not duplication. He says, "One can imagine a computer simulation of ... the action of digestive processes in the stomach when it is digesting pizza. And the simulation is no more the real thing in the case of the brain as it is in the case of ... the stomach. Barring miracles ... you could not digest pizza by running a program that simulates such digestion."[52] This is a serious attack on strong AI that is difficult to refute; many people have tried.

Maybe we want to make an electric car that behaves like a petrol car. We program a computer to simulate the operation of an internal-combustion engine and control an electric motor according to the simulation. It can even have a complex audio system for making the right noises. Searle's argument is that it does not run by exploding petrol. In fact, however good the simulation, you still connect it to an electrical recharge plug

52 John R. Searle, 'Is the Brain's Mind a Computer Program?' *Scientific American* 262 (1) (1990): 26–31. PMID 2294583.

rather than filling the tank with petrol.[53] The question then arises: Does it matter? An artificial mind may have the same, albeit simulated, mental states as a real mind. It may think that it is conscious. If so, how can we deny it?

However, the picture is even more confused because we never know what the mind is thinking; we only know what it tells us it is thinking. If it says 'I am alive,' do we have to believe it? After all it is trivial to make a computer say that. Even being able to see what it is thinking won't help if the mind itself does not know if it is really conscious or just duplicating consciousness.

Disinformation

There is a story of two monks who, journeying through a mountain pass, were caught in a storm. They struggled towards a light and found themselves in a castle. The lord who lived there made them comfortable. He wined and dined them and sent them to bed in fine bedrooms. Throughout the whole evening they were terrified because they recognized him as an infamously cruel man who tortured and murdered for the pleasure of it. The next morning they came down to breakfast and he asked them both, 'How do my people think of me? Do they love me or hate me?' The first monk, fearing to tell the

---

53 To head off the pedants, yes, you could give it a steam turbine that was powered by petrol and generated electricity. But the mileage you got would depend on the turbine, not the simulated engine. There would still be differences.

truth, said that the lord's people loved him. The second monk, to whom a lie was anathema, said that the lord's people hated him. The lord then killed one monk and let the other go on his way. The question is, Which monk did he kill?

This is known as a disinformation problem. There is no right answer and the response we give to it depends more on our own beliefs than on any external evidence. We know the lord is cruel and sadistic but we are told nothing of his sense of honour or narcissism that might allow us to make a reasoned choice. We form a model of the man in our mind using our own biases and beliefs and consider how that model would react. (This is, in itself, an interesting insight into the function of the mind.)

So it is with the question of thinking machines. As yet, we have no external evidence for the manner by which consciousness arises in the brain. Even thinking too deeply about it being a mechanistic mirage can be disturbingly uncomfortable. All we have are our intuition and faith. Nobody knows how and why the sense of conscious identity, which says, 'I think, therefore I am,' is created in the human brain. Those who have absolute faith in the physics and the maths believe it must be an emergent property of the right programs; if we create the software, the consciousness will appear because, they believe, physics and maths is all that can possibly be in the human brain.

Back before 1995, home computers used an operating system called DOS. Programs written for DOS do not work on modern machines; the hardware and the operating system have changed too much. However, there is a product called

DOSBOX[54] that you can run on any computer, which simulates not only the DOS operating system but also the computer chip it ran on and the video and audio cards around at the time. That takes a lot of computing power, of course, but as we saw above computing power has increased exponentially. A reasonably modern PC can run the old software at the same speed that it is designed to run. So far as the software is concerned, it is running on a 70MHz Pentium[55] with the hardware interfaces it expects to see, although we now see its output in a window on our desktop. Is the program running any less in DOSBOX than when it is running on a real Pentium PC?

So far as we can tell, the human brain is an organ for processing information. We can understand everything it does as flows and transformations of data. It takes input from the senses and the endocrine system and it produces outputs to the muscles. Unlike Searle's example of the digestive system, we don't need to simulate anything; we can implement the same data processing in a computer.

When we listen to a recording of a piece of music on a CD, the sound waves have been transformed to electrical impulses, those have been converted to sequences of numbers encoded as microscopic pits in a piece of plastic, transformed again into distortions of laser light, back into numbers, into electrical impulses and finally back into sound. While the recording is

54 It's free software. See www.dosbox.com
55 Pentium is a trademark of Intel.

never perfect, it can be as close to it as one cares to make it. The music is still music, even though at times it does not exist as sound waves. Similarly, there seems no reason to suspect that thoughts will cease to be thoughts just because they are not electrochemical signals in nerve cells.

Even if it is possible theoretically to reproduce a human brain in a computer, we may not understand enough about the structure and operation of the brain to do so. We don't presently have the technology to map every single neuron and we don't know exactly how they differ from one another. It seems likely that, given sufficient time, we will eventually learn enough to do so. Even then, reproducing a brain is not the same as creating a mind from scratch. That requires a whole different set of discoveries.

It is a cliché that whenever an artificial intelligence researcher is asked when we will get human-like robots, the answer is always five to 20 years; they've been giving the same answer now for over half a century. We are getting closer all the time but it is still possible that there may be problems that take much longer to solve. Nevertheless, we are getting closer. Pretty soon we will be close enough for all practical purposes and even if we don't create a conscious robot, the reasons for our failure will change our world.

CHAPTER 17

Singularity

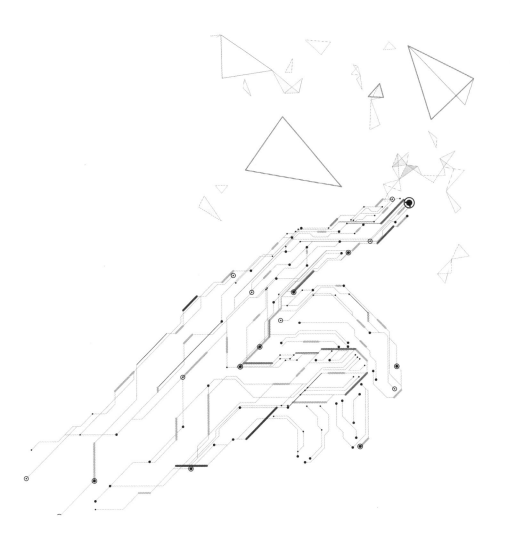

If one studies artificial intelligence for long enough, one will encounter the concept of the Singularity. This apocalyptic event, it is said, is just around the corner and will either wipe out the human race or change us into semi-robotic entities with powers we cannot even imagine. It has been called the Rapture of the Nerds, pointing out its similarity to the Rapture that some Christian groups believe will precede the Second Coming of Christ and cause all righteous people to disappear from the face of the Earth in the twinkling of an eye.[56] It certainly has the same flavour.

If AI became a threat...

The Singularity has been postulated for as long as people have been concerned about machines. In its modern form it is proposed to occur when machine intelligence exceeds human intelligence. At that time, it is said, machines will be able to program themselves to be more intelligent still, and those will continue designing smarter machines and so on, until humans are left as far beneath them as ants are below us. The more friendly interpretation has humans becoming increasingly inter-connected to machines (even now it is near impossible to do

56 See I Corinthians 15:52.

school homework without the Internet) until we are indistinguishable from machines or achieve such an increase in our abilities that we are unimaginably powerful.

In an even more catastrophic vision we don't have a robot that is designing robots but simply one that is refining its own programming as a means to optimize some task it has been given. Let's say it is a housemaid. One day, when it has optimized itself to be much more intelligent than a human, it decides that the house would be much cleaner if it killed off all the messy humans. Since it is so smart, it can do so sneakily without anyone catching on until it is too late.

The final version is, of course, where robots become conscious and for one reason or another declare war on the human race.

Technological acceleration

It isn't the success of recent advances in artificial intelligence that has given rise to these concerns. In a recent DARPA challenge[57] robots had to drive a car, open a door, turn a valve, operate a hand-drill, unplug and replug an electrical cable, walk over some rubble and climb a short flight of steps. If we were being generous we might say a human could complete the course in a minute. The winning robot took more than 40 minutes. Rather the proponents of the Singularity point to the

---

57 The DARPA robotics challenge is an annual competition. The description is of the 2015 event. See http://www.theroboticschallenge.org/

exponential acceleration of all forms of technology, especially computing power.

When we look at a graph of exponential growth it always looks scary. There is an almost flat section behind us where life seems to be more or less sedentary but we are sitting right at a sharp kink where progress suddenly shoots upwards at an ever-increasing rate. However, it is important to realize that the graph always looks like that. When the scale is chosen to show progress the clearest we are always just about to experience that sudden upward surge. But if the graph had been drawn 20 years ago it would have looked exactly the same, and we have survived so far. The future is certain to bring changes, just as the recent past has seen the rise of the Internet and mobile phones. Whereas 50 years ago people would go straight from school to the job that they would hold until retirement, now jobs are more transitory; 20 years ago there was no such thing as a web designer. As technology advances we will have to adapt to its ever-increasing rate of change. There will be challenges: people will get left behind; employment rates may fall; ever-shorter-lived occupations may have ever-higher skill requirements. Technology will fill the gaps, training and supporting new workers while carrying out the menial tasks that people used to do.

We cannot say what that new technology will be; we see only five or ten years ahead and there is inertia that is not taken into account by the rate of progress. We have the technology now to give everyone high-speed monorails but the existing infrastructure would need to be ripped up and completely replaced, which would cost more than we are able to pay. There have been several designs for flying cars but the necessary requirement of getting a pilot's licence and obeying air traffic regulations has made them uneconomic to mass-produce.

In the next few decades, computers will have the same power as the human brain. When that time comes we might expect that Weak AI will give us computers and robots that at least approach human abilities – but we cannot be certain of that. They might be able to research artificial intelligence themselves and gradually become more intelligent than us. It's unlikely to happen overnight, though, and it may never happen. Intelligence is not a simple concept. Maybe the super-brains might be able to do mathematics faster than any human but that does not mean they would be super humanly capable orators or medical diagnosticians. Some skills may still take a lifetime to acquire.

There is nothing mystical about an intelligent computer that makes it able to create successors that are cleverer than humans. The techniques that we have now, such as neural networks and genetic algorithms, are already capable of tasks that we do not know how to do ourselves. Such programs have been impacting our lives for several years. It is widely accepted that the stock market is more volatile because computers are making large numbers of trades thousands of times quicker than humans are able to.[58]

58 See Adam Shell, '7 Reasons the Stock Market is So Volatile', *USA Today*, 11 August, 2011, accessed 19 January, 2016, http://usatoday30.usatoday.com/money/perfi/stocks/2011-08-10-volatile-markets_n.htm

We already have brain-to-machine interfaces. Cochlear implants have been used to restore a measure of hearing to profoundly deaf people since 1957. A microphone picks up the ambient sounds and its signal is processed and passed to electrodes in the inner ear. From the original single channel, allowing the patient to distinguish rhythm but nothing else, modern implants have more than 20 channels. While this is a significant advance, it could not be described as normal hearing. To get some feel for what it means, imagine listening to a tune played on a piano on which less than one-quarter of the keys worked and the ones that did were out of tune.

Cochlear implants were relatively simple because the nerve endings that need to be stimulated are available and easily accessed in the inner ear. Similarly, the nerve cells that provide vision are arranged on the retina of the eye and some cases of blindness can be treated with a retinal implant. Just as in the case of hearing, the resolution of the restored sight is limited. In the initial trials patients' sight improved from 'blind' to 'low sight'. They can see lights and some degree of shape. They reported being able to tell the direction a road ran by identifying the street lights.

Prosthetic limbs can also be controlled by measuring activity in muscles or nerve fibres and translating that signal into movements of the artificial limb. The first such devices used stomach muscles as proxies. By tensing individual muscles a robotic arm could be controlled. Researchers are now trying to take signals from the nerves that used to control the lost arm. Current prosthetic hands do little more than open and shut the fingers. The user can change the type of grip so that the fingers close in a different pattern but not control each finger separately. There is also no feedback to the user. There is no sensation that might feel pain or just the degree of pressure being exerted on a held object. There is no obvious reason for those to be impossible though. Ongoing research and miniaturization should produce a limb that works at least as well as the one it replaces. We are unlikely to see one that works better, simply due to the laws of physics. A strong arm requires a strong attachment to a robust skeleton, and more power needs heavier batteries.

Before long it will be possible to connect thousands of neurons to a single implanted device. This will allow ear and eye implants to provide much the same experience as the organs they replace. It may even be possible to control a limb using an interface implanted in the brain. Even so, it is doubtful that healthy individuals would volunteer for major brain surgery involving an infection with a virus that puts algae genes into their brain cells.[59] There are many diseases and disabilities that could be treated by such technology; such an implant could be used by sufferers of Alzheimer's or Parkinson's disease. But very few would consider such an operation just to make them better at work or play until the surgery becomes entirely routine. That's

---

59 This appears to be the most likely method of connecting to a large number of individual neurons. The algae genes cause the neurons to make substances that light up when the neuron fires and also make it sensitive to light so it can be switched on or off with light. Up to now electrodes have been used to interface with individual neurons but the brain sees them as foreign bodies and creates scar tissue around them. After a while they stop working.

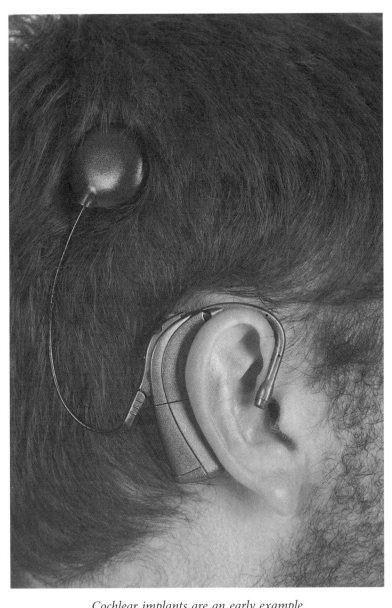

Cochlear implants are an early example
of a successful brain-to-machine interface.

not going to happen soon. Most of us will have to be content with the bodies and brains we already have.

How likely is a single intelligence to turn on humans?

A single artificial intelligence that was programmed to improve its own abilities might be so successful at doing so that it caused a major catastrophe. Maybe it is tasked with making paper clips and its goal is to make as many as it can as fast as possible. To start with it would optimize its own mechanism and programming to be efficient but then it would realize that there are a lot of machines elsewhere in the world that are not making paper clips. If it learned enough it might be able to subvert those machines to help it. That would be annoying enough but it might decide that humans who were trying to stop it were getting in the way and must be disposed of. In the apocalyptic version of this narrative, the AI becomes so smart that it can out-think the humans that are trying to stop it. It becomes the perfect liar and the perfect con-artist. Before its operators are aware that anything has gone wrong it subverts a genetics laboratory to create a deadly virus that wipes out the human race. With no limitations on it any more it expands until all of the planet's resources are employed making paper clips, except for the ones making the interstellar spaceships that will flood the universe looking for more planets to convert to making more paper clips.

Like the other scenarios, this one is plausible only in certain circumstances. The machine must be powerful enough to implement this super-intelligence and it must understand how to lie convincingly without being empathic enough to recognize that humans have value or insightful enough to realize that one can have too many paperclips. It will be some time before computing resources are cheap enough that we can carelessly provide so much for such a trivial task and if the job required high intelligence the operators would be more likely to notice if the intelligence started to order nerve gas.

It is far more likely that this scenario will play on a smaller stage. For instance a military robot might decide that the best way to clear out all the terrorists in a village is to kill everyone. That would be a tragedy and a major international incident, but it wouldn't be the end of the human race.

The likelihood of the Singularity, just like that of conscious machines, is a disinformation problem. We do not know enough yet to let us decide whether it is a significant danger or not. Nevertheless, at some future time, be it 20 years or 100, we will have machines that are indistinguishable from living, thinking beings. They will be at least as intelligent as we are and they might be much smarter. Just as with any new technology, dangers, opportunities and ethical questions will arise but we will have to wait a while longer before we can argue about them in concrete terms.

Even safe AI is dangerous

Current artificial intelligence appears to be better than it actually is. People trust it more than they should. We saw this with the

Eliza chat-bot but there it was safe enough. Years ago drivers were needing to be rescued by the Fire Service because they trusted what their sat-nav devices told them to do and they ended up in fields or driving into rivers. Adding artificial intelligence increases the likelihood that people will blindly believe what they are told. For example ChatGPT (version 3.0 at the time of writing) sounds very convincing. It can turn its hand to many different types of text.

Several magazines publishing Science Fiction short stories have stopped accepting submissions that they have not asked for because they are being swamped by stories written by ChatGPT. The stories are terrible, ChatGPT is about as good as a poor fan-fiction author, but it was taking too much time to weed them out.

A lawyer may lose his license and his career because he asked ChatGPT for cases that supported the position he wanted to take in court. ChapGPT provided several case citations and he used them in documents he submitted to the court. He did not realise that ChatGPT has no concept of truth; it simply creates text that looks good. It generally produces truth because, from what it has seen, those words would be more plausible than anything else. In this example though, there were no cases that supported his position. Therefore it had to invent ones that did. There was no way to tell that it had done so except to research the cases — which every lawyer should do every time, no matter if the citations were provided by AI or a trusted colleague.[60]

60 For a full and easy to understand analysis of this legal disaster, I recommend the Legal Eagle video: https://www.youtube.com/watch?v=oqSYljRYDEM

In conclusion

Artificial intelligence is a difficult field to predict. When the first robot cars drove on empty roads in 1986, one might have supposed that most of the difficulties had been overcome, and yet eight years later they still depended on human drivers to handle unexpected situations. Even in 2015, the Google self-driving cars did not understand temporary traffic lights and depended on inch-perfect maps of the area in which they are operating. The whole field is the same, gradually solving issues one by one, first in the simple cases and then becoming more and more generalized. Until those first problems are solved the next ones are unknown. So we can never say with any certainty how close we are to a solution, but every year we get a little closer. I will quote Alan Turing one last time: "We can only see a short distance ahead, but we can see plenty there that needs to be done."[61]

61 A.M. Turing, 'Computing Machinery and Intelligence', Mind: A Quarterly Review of Psychology and Philosophy (October 1950): 433–60. The paper is available in several places on the Internet, including in the Mind back-catalogue at http://mind.oxfordjournals.org/; or try the Loebner Prize website at http://www.loebner.net/Prizef/TuringArticle.html. The paper is readable and thought provoking: I recommend interested readers to search it out.

INDEX

PICTURE CREDITS